£1.50

THE WOMAN GOLFER

THE
WOMAN·GOLFER
A LIFETIME OF GOLFING SUCCESS

Belle Robertson
AND
Lewine Mair

MAINSTREAM
PUBLISHING

First published in Great Britain in 1988 by
MAINSTREAM PUBLISHING COMPANY (EDINBURGH) LTD
7 Albany Street
Edinburgh EH1 3UG
ISBN 1 85158 0689 (cloth)

British Library Cataloguing in Publication Data

Mair, Lewine
    The Woman Golfer: A Lifetime of Golfing Success
    1. Golf
    I. Title   II. Robertson, Belle
796.352'3   GV965

Typeset in 12 on 12½ pt Baskerville by Blackwood Pillans & Wilson Ltd.
Printed in Great Britain by Billings & Sons, Worcester.

Contents

Chapter 1

A Backward Glance

January 2, 1987. I am on the long drive back from my childhood home on the Mull of Kintyre to Glasgow. In the past, my thoughts on this annual winter's journey would have been of the coming season, of the golfing goals I was setting myself.

This year, I remind myself, there is no season ahead, the reason being that I retired from serious competitive golf at the end of 1986. But this is one New Year when I am happy enough to look back rather than forward. I always wanted to have something special in my record book before I would retire and, to my great joy, 1986 was a year in which I matched the targets I had set myself.

I can remember, vividly, my thoughts at the start of '86. They were of the Curtis Cup, a biennial match between Great Britain and Ireland and the Americans and an occasion which, in the world of women's golf, supersedes all others.

The match was to be held at Prairie Dunes in Kansas and I knew, only too well, that if, at the age of 50, I wanted to be considered for a place in the eight-strong Great Britain and Ireland side, I had to get myself 100 per cent fit and win another major title. I had won the British Women's Stroke-Play championship at Formby in September '85 but, had the selectors not wanted me in their side, it would have been all too easy for them to dismiss that last title with a ''but that was last year'' explanation. The event on which I set my sights was the Scottish Women's championship at St Andrews which was to be played just three weeks before the Curtis Cup selectors were due to announce their team.

Soon after I returned home, I wrote away to Tip Anderson, the St Andrews caddie whose name will always be associated with that of Arnold Palmer. Tip is a wonderful man and I was asking him if he would be good enough to caddie for me. His reply was one which gave exactly the right lift to my practice and training sessions on those dark January days. ''Of course I'll caddie for you,'' he said. ''I always enjoy caddying for a winner.''

I felt a lot of pressure when it came to the week of the championship but, from the start, Tip never allowed me to think that I wasn't going to win. I tell elsewhere of how, having gone four up after four holes in my final against Gullane's Lesley Hope, I was brought back to square at the 11th. The 12th was a particularly traumatic hole in that I had to make a six-footer to stay level. However, patience and long hours of practice paid off and in the end I won by three and two.

There had been something special about my first win in the Scottish—in 1965 at Nairn—in that when you win a major title for a first time, there is the sneaking feeling that it could just spell the beginning of a career at the highest levels. In all, I won the Scottish championship seven times but to win at St Andrews, in a year when I felt I had no option but so to do, left me in such a state of elation that I could not sleep for two nights.

When it came to the Curtis Cup, Diane Bailey, our captain, had the same gift as Tip Anderson for imbuing in her players the feeling that they had it in them to win. Diane and her vice-captain, Elsie Brown, left no stone unturned in fulfilling their respective roles and, in response to the example they set, the players were intent on giving more than they had ever given before. We knew in our heart of hearts that if we were to fail, it was simply that we were not good enough. There was no time at which Diane sat us down and told us we were the better side. It was something she got across almost in throw-away lines.

I have played in international teams across four decades and I recognised that this '86 Great Britain and Ireland side had that mixture of qualities for which no one can plan. It is a mixture which, given the time and situation, is just there. To me, our girls had exactly the right brand of cheek, drive and desire.

The selectors had based the team on the one which had won the Vagliano Trophy in Germany the previous October and, by the time of the Curtis Cup, we had built up a great friendship and trust in one another. It goes without saying that, when we succeeded in winning the Curtis Cup for the first time in 30 years, our mood was one of unparalleled delight.

Trish Johnson and Lillian Behan have since moved on to the professional scene and other members of that side may do the

A full swing in a mini-skirt. Practising at Douglas Park in the '70s.

same but, for me, the winning of that match represented the perfect stepping-stone to retirement, the right moment to go.

In dwelling on the end of my career, my thoughts inevitably flash back to the beginnings . . .

Early Days

There was a lot of excitement in the countryside in which my brother, Dan, and I were brought up, much of it not fully appreciated by me until I left. But that excitement was tempered by a certain degree of austerity. At our home, Eden Farm, we had

3

no electric lights and no central heating until 1954, while there was no regular bus at the end of the road.

As is the case with most small communities, the people of Southend have always made their own entertainment and in my youth that entertainment revolved almost wholly around the school and the church. You could be a member of the church choir, the Gaelic choir and, if you were so inclined, the local drama group. By way of sporting recreation, the boys would have football in the winter and Highland games—tossing the caber, races and tugs-of-war—in the summer. They would play golf all the year round, as would the girls in that, apart from the athletics we would do at school, there was nothing else for us to play.

Both the local hotels, the Keil and the Argyll Arms, had tennis courts, but these were only for the use of hotel guests. I myself was keen on school games and, though not very good at the high jump, was a pretty efficient sprinter. Indeed I have often thought that, had it not been for golf, I could happily have been an athlete.

Campbeltown Grammar School was divided into four groups or houses which took their names from the surrounding areas—Davaar, Kilbrannan, Ben Guilion and Knockscalbert. I was in Kilbrannan and I can remember a sports day when, after I had had my first success in the 100 yards sprint and the master standing by the tape asked me for my name and house, I made a reply, the memory of which makes me redden to this day: ''Belle McCorkindale, Eden Farm''

It is a tale which brings to mind a time at Sunday school when John McVicar, on holiday from university, was standing in for his father, the Reverend Angus John McVicar, or ''Old Mac'', as he was affectionately known by all of us. We always had little cards, little texts, that we had to learn each week and, in going over what we had supposedly memorised from the previous session, John McVicar asked, ''Who lived in the Garden of Eden?'' ''Belle and Dan,'' returned a small voice from the class.

Initially there were two churches in Southend, the High church and the Low church. The two were so called not so much for ecclesiastical reasons as that the High church stood above and outside the village where the Low church was tucked in among the houses.

Those were the days in which the local tinker families, the McPhees and the Townsleys being the usual names, would take their babies to St Blaans, the High church, to get them christened by ''Old Mac''. Following the ceremony, Mrs McVicar, a lovely,

4

plump lady, would give the party tea and follow the old tradition of handing over pieces of silver for luck. The tinkers would thank everyone very kindly before proceeding to the manse at the Low church. There they would ring at the doorbell and ask the Reverend Tolmie to perform the same ceremony so they could have some more tea and some more silver.

The clubhouse at Dunaverty which was replaced in the mid-seventies by something along rather more modern lines. I feel greatly honoured to have been asked to be the honorary captain when the club celebrates its centenary in 1989.

5

Many of the tinker children eventually attended our local school and, to give some indication of just how unused they were to even the simple sophistication of a Southend school dinner, there was one marvellous day when a young boy, confronted by a wobbling jelly, turned tail and fled.

When it became uneconomic to have two churches and two ministers, the High church and the Low joined forces. For a time there would be a service in each on alternate Sundays but, eventually, they settled on the church in the best state of repair—namely, St Blaans. "Old Mac" was the minister for a long, long time. He had grey wispy hair combed over the top of his head and, at Bible classes, would walk up and down with his hands tucked in his clerical vest when he was not using them to make a point. Having spent the quarter of an hour in which we were meant to be preparing the hall standing in the belfry and daring one another to give the bell a tug, the girls would settle in the front left pew and the boys in the right for these gentle little lectures from which we learnt so much. Spiritually, I have always felt "Old Mac", whose other son, Angus, is the well-known author and whose grandson, Jock, writes on golf in the *Scottish Daily Express*, got us off on the right foot.

I must have been 15 or 16 when my mother, who shared my belief that I was essentially an "outdoor" person as opposed to one destined to sit behind a desk for ever more, arranged for me to have a course of golf lessons from Hector Thomson at Machrihanish. My brother had started two years earlier, my father having encouraged him to concentrate on golf rather than football because he worried lest a footballing injury might interfere with his work on the farm.

The first golf clubs we had were given to us by my mother's cousin and, with these lying around the house, we got into the way of hitting stones across the farmyard and golf balls in the fields. As was always the case, I would tag along after Dan. I could therefore play a bit when I turned up at Machrihanish and, looking back, I have the feeling that Hector Thomson noticed straightaway that I had a certain amount of aptitude.

I fell in love with the man on my first visit. He was tall, stately and a first-class gentleman. Though women golfers of that time were still being judged according to how attractively they swung and it was considered somewhat unseemly to have to go searching for a ball in rough up to the waist, Hector encouraged me from the start to hit the ball as if I hated it. And that, I must say, was the

6

way I liked to play. He built up a great understanding with all his pupils, although I cannot resist recalling that memorable occasion when he could scarcely have been described as being on the same wavelength as one Janet McNaughton.

Janet, a past captain of Dunbartonshire, was clearly impressed by the way in which Hector was so quick, so to speak, to get to the bottom of her problems. ''Ben, sit doon; ben, sit doon,'' was the instruction he kept reiterating. Janet duly flexed her knees and sat down a little more at the address. But still Hector was not satisfied, persisting, ever more pressingly, with the same line in advice. The lesson was nearing its end and Janet was practically sitting on the grass when suddenly she realised that he had not been speaking to her at all. He had simply been exhorting his dog, Ben, to stop running round.

With Hector Thomson, the man who started me off in golf. Hector was 90 at the time this picture was taken but was still taking a lively interest in my game.

7

My early lessons came at a time when all my school exams, so long the bane of my existence, were over. The system in those days was that if you did not pass the various tests, you were kept down. I had never particularly enjoyed school work and I never did much homework but, when the hour drew near for those exams, my competitive instincts would surface and I would do a lot of cramming. Each year I managed to escape disgrace by going up, but there were long weeks when I would live in fear and trepidation whilst waiting for the results.

From school, I would catch the bus to Machrihanish for my golf lesson before returning to Campbeltown to catch the school bus home. On a Saturday, I would have to walk a mile and a half from the farm in order to catch a bus to Stewarton and I would then have to catch another to the golf course. My father would sometimes come and fetch me, but there was never any question of his taking me as well. I probably thought it hard at the time—especially on those occasions when the car was sitting in the garage—but, looking back, it was a good discipline.

At the end of a lesson, Hector, who was by then no longer playing himself, would encourage me to go out and have a game with the clubmaster, a retired miner by name of Jimmy Kerr. Jimmy, like Hector, was one of the finest men you could hope to meet. He was a wonderfully natural striker of a golf ball and I picked up a lot simply from playing alongside him. Also, where Hector concentrated on technical issues, Jimmy guided my thinking to no small extent, stressing the importance of taking my time over each shot. He always had words of encouragement to offer before I went away to compete and I shall never forget how, on the occasion of my first tournament—the British Girls' at West Kilbride—he sent a box of chocolates.

When he was 66 Jimmy Kerr went round in 66; when 67, in 67. In fact, I cannot remember a year when he did not equal his age. There was a delightful rivalry between himself and Ellis Knowles, an American who used to come over in the summer and who was similarly adept at playing to his age. As I remember it, I was with Mr Knowles on the day he matched his 72 years.

Another thing I can recall about Ellis Knowles was of a stay in which he took on a local lad as his caddie. At the start of the week, he had asked of the boy what he intended doing with the money he would save. The youngster replied that he would be putting it towards a new bicycle. Knowles said nothing at the time but, when it came to the end of the week, he upped the final payment to the point where the boy would be able to make his purchase.

There were plenty of other visitors to Machrihanish with whom I used to play and I well remember Jimmy Kerr and I taking on such celebrated players as Wilbur Muirhead, a future captain of the R. & A. and the McLeod brothers from Ranfurly.

The club certainly had its share of characters with, among them, Hector Thomson's son-in-law, Bob Dobbie. Bob hardly swung as his father-in-law would have wished, but he had a quick wit to go with his quick and somewhat less than rhythmic swing.

The first tee at Machrihanish used to be surrounded by a fence and, as you walked off the tee, you had to go through a little gate. There was a notice asking you to keep it shut but, on the day I am recalling, it was the Spring meeting and, with so many people teeing off, there was no point in closing it every time. When Bob Dobbie's turn came to tee up, he took an almighty thrash at the ball and sent it scuttling through the said gate. With this being the Spring meeting, those watching did not like to laugh. Dobbie, though, wasted no time in breaking their embarrassed silence. "Who the hell," he asked, "left the gate open?"

There were two policemen—Crae McIntyre and Alan Mackenzie—with whom I enjoyed many a round, while Dick Gillion was another well-known local of whom I have fond memories. He lived in the woods on the far side of the village and the story goes that, towards the end of his life, he would simply cut down a tree, drag one end into his fire and push it further and further in as it burned. A good golfer, he was at one stage almost always to be found up at the club. No doubt he was making his way there on the day he bumped into Captain Taylor, the owner of the Keil Hotel. Captain Taylor stopped to talk to him, but you could sense that the two hotel guests he had with him were eyeing Dick somewhat disapprovingly. At the same moment, a family of tinkers appeared on the scene.

"Are these some more of your local inhabitants?" queried one of the guests.

"No," replied Dick, looking the man straight in the eye, "just common summer visitors such as yourselves."

Apart from all the good people I have mentioned, I have always felt I owed a great deal to my old Southend school headmaster, John Cameron. When we came to our last year, he gave us a number of chats about what we should expect when we went to Campbeltown Grammar School. The one topic to which he would always return was of how each of us should appreciate that our character was particularly precious, that it was something we must think very seriously about at all times. In addition, there were a couple of lines—and I have never found out where they came from—he liked to recite:

> Do not follow where the path may lead
> Go instead where there is no path and leave a trail.

Those words stuck. Every time I left Kintyre I wanted to return, having done just that.

Even though the local people did not put any kind of pressure on me, I hated going back from a county match or a championship if I had lost. But oh! the joy of that long drive home on those occasions when I had won.

When two heads are better than one . . .

One area in which the professionals are so lucky is that they can experiment with different clubs without having to foot the bill. But, difficult though it may be, financially, for the amateur to follow suit, I think there is a definite case for having two putters.

Your average green in these islands asks for a putter-head with a touch of loft but, in moving on to slick championship greens, a lighter, straighter-faced implement will serve rather better.

Unfortunately, the fact that we putt so often on greens that are so far removed from championship standard does nothing to help to make us a nation of good putters. We fail to develop the touch and feel acquired by those who do all their putting on good greens.

If you feel that your putting is totally bereft of this touch and feel, one of the best places to discover it is on your carpet at home. Indeed, Michael Bonallack was so convinced of this that he would never purchase a carpet without first considering its putting qualities. Arnold Palmer used to put down a dollar and try and stop the ball on it. I have tried this to good effect with my Scottish pound note and, if you would like to be able to cope with the kind of lightning fast greens they get in the Masters at Augusta, you had best do the same!

Ellis Knowles, myself, Jimmy Kerr and Crae McIntyre preparing to tee off at the first at Machrihanish.

Golf for beginners . . .

It was during the summer of '71 and Suzanne Cadden, who was to win the World Junior championship in 1973, Maureen Walker and I were on the practice ground at Clydebank and District G.C. where our lesson from Elliot Rowan was nearing its end. Since the next pupil, a middle-aged lady, was approaching, Elliot suggested that we should each hit two or three shots with a five iron by way of a closing exercise. I hit my three first and, having caught each as well as I know how, moved across to pass the time of day with the new arrival. Her opening gambit, however, was not quite what I had expected.

"Are you a beginner, too?" she asked.

British debut. The 1959 Vagliano Trophy match at Wentworth.

Chapter 2

Spreading My Wings

For the first couple of my golfing years, I never played anywhere other than Dunaverty or Machrihanish. Quite simply, there was nowhere else to play. However, there came a day when I was brought in on a discussion in which two ladies were planning their annual outing to the open meeting at Dunoon. They knew I would be interested and suggested I should ask at home if I could accompany them for the two-day trip. As the crow flies—and that would be over the Kilbrannan Sound, the Isle of Arran and the Sound of Bute—the journey is one of about 60 miles. By car, though, it is a winding 250 miles or so.

I looked forward to that open meeting for weeks and, when the day came, I did an 81 less 14. It won the handicap prize and was only a shot away from being the best scratch score. As for my prize, that was a £5 voucher which was pretty generous in those days.

For many years my mother had been trying to encourage me to go with her on one of her occasional trips to Glasgow and it was in June of the following year that I relented, saying I would go if I could spend my voucher. We set off in the car and, as we drove through Campbeltown, we met a lady who was the nurse to Sir John Stirling Maxwell of Pollock House. She was back on holiday in Kintyre and gratefully accepted our offer of a lift along the main road to her house. My mother was talking about our trip to Glasgow and mentioned how I was hoping to buy some golf clubs. Whereupon this good lady chipped in with the suggestion that we should head first for Crawleys in Union Street.

The assistant who came forward to serve us in Crawleys was a little taken aback when I eliminated each club in turn on the grounds that it was "too light". Feeling more than a little exasperated, she went in search of some new "Jean Donalds" which, she regretted, were rather expensive. I told her I liked them very much but again made the point that they were too light.

Over in the corner of the shop I had noticed people knocking balls into a golf net and I asked if I might be allowed to have a go. This, apparently, was not common practice with the new clubs, but she advised us to come back in half an hour, during which time she would have a word with the manager. Permission was duly granted and, still wearing my best Harris Tweed suit, I took hold of one of the clubs and swished some balls into the net. The volley of questions detonated by those shots had nothing to do with whether or not I liked the clubs. "What's your handicap?" asked the assistant before adding, almost in the same breath, "Where do you come from?" On learning that we were staying overnight, she offered to take me for a round the next day over Douglas Park, her home course.

Her name was Joan Weston and it turned out that she was an active member of the Dunbartonshire county side who knew everyone who was anyone in the world of county golf. We were joined, for our game, by a Mrs Scott, the captain of Lanarkshire. Except for putting, I did everything right, going round in 80 or 81. But what had them talking rather more than my scoring was the distance I could hit the ball. There were certain greens I had hit in two which they had never seen reached before.

My stay on what I always tended to see as the mainland lasted a further day as Joan Weston arranged for me to go to West Kilbride to play with the legendary Jean McCulloch. I knew the name for, on our first night in Glasgow, the uncle with whom we were staying had talked of her as his particular heroine. It was a thrilling experience for me but, as luck would have it, I started off by all but hitting my opening tee shot into the gardens on the right—a difficult thing to do—and generally played as badly on that second day as I had played well the day before.

Miss McCulloch obviously had rather more faith in me than I had in myself at that point and suggested I should come and play in the British Girls' championship which was to be staged at West Kilbride in September of that year. She found an entrance form and, at the same time, arranged for me to have accommodation with the lady captain, a Mrs Cohen, who lived at the far end of the course.

Two days before the championship, the Girls Golfing Society of Great Britain, as they were called, had their annual medal event for past and present competitors in the British Girls'. I had no

14

idea what kind of scores people would be handing in but, to my amazement, I went off that evening with the scratch cup. What is more, since I had played so well, I found myself nominated for the junior Scotland side to meet England the following day.

Nowadays, all of the home countries play each other but, at that stage, it was purely an England–Scotland affair. Scotland lost 7–1, the one point having come from my win over a girl I have never heard of since—namely, Jacqueline Mitton from Dore and Totley. The score had been six and five and, as we walked back to the clubhouse, I was approached by a reporter. This was my first ever meeting with a journalist and it maybe goes a long way towards explaining why, for years after, the press thought of me as being a pretty awkward customer.

He asked me where I came from and how I contrived to hit the ball so much further than everyone else. I, in turn, gave him a straightforward account of how I came from Kintyre where I worked on the family farm. To him, it was a little out of the ordinary and so carried away did he get in penning his story of faraway farms that he introduced a herd of ''prize-winning'' cattle. When my father read the paper the next day he was appalled that I had so elevated his herd. Nothing I could say would convince him that I had never mentioned anything of the sort and, as a result, I thereafter did not dare to give any more of myself to a reporter other than to say yes or no.

The only other time I can recall actually running into trouble with a reporter was after Maurice Moir and I had won the Sunningdale Foursomes in 1960. I had been hoping I might be in with a chance of making the Curtis Cup side that year, but imagine my horror when this particular golf writer quoted me as having said, ''Surely, I must get in the team now''. I hadn't said that any more than I had talked of prize-winning cattle but, embarrassing though that was for me, the newspaper did not respond to my request for a correction.

Anyhow, back to the British Girls' championship where, having been lucky enough to distinguish myself in the preliminaries, I found myself up against England's first reserve in the first round of the championship proper. In my innocence, I felt that that meant I should win. As you will have guessed, I was beaten. And that was when I began to realise that golf was maybe not so easy after all.

In the meantime, my friend Joan Weston was working behind the scenes to get me involved in county golf. It was more than a little difficult to draw someone from Kintyre into the fold in that Argyll did not have a county team. There was the suggestion that I should become a member of Cardross in order to qualify to play for Dunbartonshire, but Dunbartonshire themselves sorted things out with the recommendation that Dunbartonshire and Argyll should do the sensible thing and join forces. They did and they are still together to this day, making what I feel to be a pretty fine county. As I glance through my record, I see that I have done none too badly on their behalf.

During the years when I was still in Kintyre, I would travel up from home on the day before a county match and spend the night with the Robertson family in Glasgow. They were a family who had come each year to Southend for their summer holidays and I had played a lot of golf with the two sons, Ian and Robert. Robert was generally considered to be the better player in that he was a long hitter who had the occasional great day. Ian, in contrast, was shorter and steadier. When Robert got married and I went to the wedding, Ian and I got to know each other a little better and when, in 1959, I reached the final of the British championship at the Berkshire and there lost to Elizabeth Price, it was Ian who rang to offer mingled commiserations and congratulations. I suspect he was among a number of people who had thought it something of a miracle that so raw a player as myself should have done so well.

He asked me out to dinner and things developed from there. To date, we have had 26 years of happy and understanding times. Very understanding, because it is not everyone who would allow you the freedom, the backing and the encouragement to go off and compete. Ian said all along that it would be futile for someone such as myself not to make the most of my talent and I would like to think that, had the situation been reversed, I could have been equally generous.

From a golfing point of view, those early trips to Glasgow were full of excitement, but I learned to sympathise with the fellows in Campbeltown who, having been all the way to Glasgow to watch their beloved Rangers getting beaten, would say, "It's an awful long road home when you've lost".

Having guided me into the county arena and enabled me to rub shoulders with such luminaries as Dorothea Sommerville and Janette Robertson, Joan Weston took it upon herself in 1955 to head me in the direction of my first Scottish championship. I didn't cover myself in glory, my golf in the middle and later '50s being best summed up by that former triple British champion and *Daily Telegraph* correspondent, Enid Wilson. Enid, whom I had met for a first time during that aforementioned British Girls' championship at West Kilbride where we were guests together in the same house, borrowed from that old children's verse to say of me: "When she is good she is very, very good and when she is bad she is horrid."

What she said rankled a little at the time, but it didn't rankle for very long. A lot of people reckoned that Enid could be a little cruel but, to me, she was only cruel to be kind. And that, in my book, is not genuine cruelty.

The chance to cheat . . .

It was in the mid-'60s and I was playing in the American Amateur at Sewickley Heights P.A. and was desperate to qualify. I had taken three putts on the eighth green and, when it came to the ninth and I left my first putt woefully short, I forgot all about the continuous putting rule and, in my anger, marked the ball and snatched it away. My playing partner, Dot Porter, seemed to assume I had done it with her little chip in mind but that was not the case. I told her so and we discussed the penalty, not knowing quite whether it was one shot or two.

It was at the 16th that Joe Dey, having heard of the goings-on, came up to us in his capacity as official referee. He asked me if I wanted details of the penalty then and there or whether I would rather wait till I was back at the clubhouse.

I said, "Tell me now", and felt my heart sink as I heard it was to be two shots. I remember thinking that that spelt the end of my qualifying chances. However, I did do something to save my score when I made a two at the 17th hole.

When we came in, Joe Dey called me across to go through the incident. He asked me if I was sure I hadn't acted with Dot's shot in mind. I reiterated that such a thought had never entered my head and my two-shot penalty was duly confirmed. To my surprise, however, I did go on to qualify, winning my first round before losing in the second to Shelley Hamlin.

Some years later, at the Curtis Cup at Lytham, I got into conversation with Joe Dey, who was by then the captain of the R. & A., beneath a portrait of Bobby Jones. We mentioned the picture at some point and he said to me, "Like you, Bobby Jones had the chance to cheat during his career and, like you, he chose not to".

What Joe Dey said that afternoon triggers a marvellous feeling of well-being every time I think about it. And I rather think that, had one chosen the other course, the legacy would have been a nagging feeling of regret.

Chapter 3

Farm-fit

I was lucky in early life; lucky to grow up in an especially beautiful corner of Scotland and to have been born into a farming family. The peace and tranquillity of Kintyre is with me still but, paradoxically, I was never less than busy. Unlike some among the city children I see here in Glasgow, who so often seem to me to be looking for something to do, I always happened upon this or that to keep me interested and amused.

I might have opened the back door with a view, perhaps, to looking for one of the cats or the dog. But, as likely as not, I would find myself caught up in the bustle of farm life. Maybe it would be someone calling across to tell me to stand at the end of the yard to stop the horses from escaping while they were at the watering trough. I would do that little job and then, almost without thinking, would follow the horses into the stables and watch the lads as they cleaned them out and put down fresh straw.

The horses were Clydesdales and, when we were little, my brother and I would play this daring game of ducking under their bellies, making sure we had chosen one of the less frisky animals. We had six of them working on the farm in my young days and they had a range of names. Ordinary names such as Polly, Bess, Mary, Jean. In which connection, I well remember a day when a traveller came to the farm and asked me what I was called. I can still hear my father interjecting, cheerfully, ''She's got a horse's name. She's called Belle!''

From the stables, I might wander across to the byre. The sheer warmth of the byre, with the breath of 50 to 60 cows, made it a wonderfully warm place to be in winter. It was the nearest we ever got to central heating.

It was a good place to work but, having said that, I must admit to having been nowhere near as enthusiastic about the cows as I was over the horses. I was always a bit scared of cows. They were big and they kicked and, when you attached them to the milking machines, they would stand on your toes. As well as that, they had horns. The Ayrshire cattle had horns with a lovely curl but the ends had the sharpest of points and you had to be careful. If they tossed their heads as you were putting the chains around their necks at feeding time, they could very easily give you a severe gash.

One of the less pleasant jobs associated with the cows was bringing in their turnips. Looking back, the turnips always seemed to me to be wet and icy and my hands would be frozen. Having wheeled them in in a barrow, I would then have to chop up a certain amount for the younger cows who didn't have strong teeth.

Milking was a dull chore and, of course, it happened twice a day. In the summer, you had to be out of your bed between five thirty and six which, to me, was a big effort. Mind you, my father and my brother were up an hour earlier in order to get the cows in from the fields. That, mercifully, was something I only had to do in the evenings.

My job at milking time was to empty the milk into a pitcher which held about three to four gallons and then carry this pitcher the 30 or 40 paces into the dairy. Having reached the dairy, I would then have to climb a small step and swing this heavy pitcher, first with my left hand and then with my right, so that the contents poured into a container at the top of the refrigerator. This in itself, when I think back, was ideal training for golf because I was working, as Gary Player says you must, with both sides of my body. What I was doing, more or less, was the equivalent of what most people do today when they go to a gymnasium, the only difference being that I was reaching this high level of fitness without really knowing.

The mental training was useful, too, in that concentration during the milking operation had to be 100 per cent. If, to give just one example, you let your attention wander, you could find the milk overflowing at the bottom of the fridge. Again, you had to be thorough. Conditions for milking were strict and, from time to time, an inspector would come round and check on the levels of hygiene. At the end of every milking session, you had to take all the utensils to bits and rinse them in cold water. Later you would wash everything properly in hot water with a soda solution. Then, finally, there was the rinsing.

Elizabeth Price with the winner's trophy—the Championship Cup—at the 1959 British Championship at The Berkshire. As the losing finalist, I am holding the Diana Fishwick Cup, while the players on either side of us, Joan Fletcher and Philomena Garvey, have the Springbok and Lion trophies which go each year to the losing semi-finalists.

Concentration . . .

One accusation I sometimes had levelled at me by sister Scots is that I don't look as if I am enjoying myself on the golf course. It is true that I don't talk or chatter when I am playing but that does not stop me enjoying myself. I am enjoying concentrating. In order to do this and because I do not like to give anything away to an opponent as to how I am reacting, I find it best to remain pretty expressionless.

My critics point to how Trevino is full of fun on the course and how Greg Norman, Seve Ballesteros and even Jack Nicklaus will have the occasional exchange with the gallery. Trevino is a case apart, but I can guarantee that the only conversation from the rest of them is conversation which requires no concentration. They will say "Good morning", "Nice day" or "How are you?" to a familiar face but they are saying it off the top of their heads. Their thoughts will never have left the task in hand.

If that is so for them—and I am certain that it is—it goes without saying that the rest of us can ill afford to get sidetracked.

The life could be very tiring and I remember occasions when, having been to a Young Farmers dance, I would step straight out of my dancing clothes into my working gear and simply lie on top of the bed. I knew that if I got between the sheets, I would never be able to get up. My father would stand and call from the bottom of the stairs. He would call once, twice and I would get away without moving. But, on the third call, I would have to roll out of bed and down the stairs. I could never have decided to take the day off, to have a long lie in. But I suspect that all the intrinsic disciplines attached to the work were to help me with the demands of tournament golf.

The first time it struck me just how fit I had been in those days was during a trip I made back to the farm a couple of years after I had got married. My sister-in-law, who had had no kind of farming upbringing at all, having worked all her life in Campbeltown, surprised me by picking up a bucket of feed-cake as if it were nothing heavier than a handbag. Out of interest, I went to pick the thing up myself and, though I had fully expected to have no more trouble than she had had, I found it heavy. That taught me a lot about how vital it is to stay with a training routine, how you can't expect to retain a skill if you don't work at it on a regular basis.

Strong though I was always considered to be in a golfing context, I decided when I was in my thirties that I would benefit from topping up the fitness that had been a legacy of my youth. I had read of how Gary Player had become a fitness fanatic and I felt that if a great player such as he was benefiting from that sort of training, it made sense for me to follow suit.

Another to inspire me in this direction was New Zealand's Bob Charles. It was in the 1972 John Player Classic, when the weather was so wet and windy that the press tent was ripped from its moorings, that a newspaper photographer caught Charles half an hour after he had come in, dripping wet, off the course. He was not, like so many others, heading for the bar. Rather, he had on his track suit and was heading back out into the rain for his evening run.

As far as I know, I was the first of the women to start training, but I could not be sure about that in that there were maybe those who, like myself, didn't talk about what they were doing. When I started, I felt as if I had got a secret weapon, something the others hadn't got.

I find it interesting to compare my preparations for the 1960

Peter Alliss, Jean Anderson, myself and Maurice Moir in the Sunningdale Foursomes, 1960.

Curtis Cup at Lindrick with those for the 1986 match at Prairie Dunes. In 1960, no one mentioned physical fitness at all. Dai Rees came to watch the match and filled our heads with good, positive thoughts, but no one spoke of our physical condition. It wouldn't have been the done thing at that time to pick out someone as being a little overweight or anything like that.

In 1986, Diane Bailey, though she did not make a big issue of it, made it abundantly clear what she wanted from us in terms of fitness. She had made a detailed study of the likely temperatures and conditions in that part of the States and how they would affect us and I remember her saying, ''I can't tell you how fit we have to be''. Though I trained all winter, I surprised myself by how well I kept up with the younger players on practice days when the

23

temperature went up to 110 degrees. In fact, it was so hot that I remember remarking to Jill Thornhill that we could have cooked meringues on the seventh fairway. On one practice day we were asked to play 27 holes. The 25th hole brought us back to the clubhouse and one group of players was greatly tempted to call it a day. Forcing oneself to turn one's back on the clubhouse and play down the 26th was a real test of character.

In the match itself, I wasn't really put to the test in that I played only foursomes. But Jill, who was then 43, came through with flying colours, winning three and a half points out of four and turning in what was possibly the best competitive performance I have ever seen. I really did admire her for it.

Especially in the later stages of my career, I found brisk walking the best way of keeping fit. Walking has been recommended to me as ''the complete exercise'' by the lady surgeon, Margaret McGregor, who had performed the hysterectomy I had had in 1976. When, while still in hospital, I had asked of her, ''How do I get fit after this?'' she had replied with an oblique observation to the effect that I would want to get fitter than most. She suggested I should start by walking as far as the nearest lamppost and back.

Having had the operation in May, there was no way in which I could do anything to rescue that season from a golfing point of view. I took things slowly and, by dint of following the surgeon's instructions, was fit enough in the September to be playing one match per day in our County Finals.

I did, I must confess, also get caught up in the jogging craze, only to have my ideas revised by Elizabeth Purcell, an Irish golfer and a physiotherapist unlucky enough to have been badly stricken by arthritis. We were talking at the British championship of 1982 at Walton Heath and she told me that at my age—I was then in my middle 40s—I was crazy to be running on pavements. I was, she said, in grave danger of jarring my knees, wearing them out. She advised cycling; so I got the bike out and used it for all sorts of trips, always making sure that I got up speed and did at least one stretch uphill. But I somehow sensed I wasn't pushing myself and so went back to walking. Particularly in the winter of '85-86, when I was anxious to give myself every chance of making the Curtis Cup, I would don a tracksuit and set off into the night, with my destination a Milngavie lamppost about one and a half miles from home. I went in all weathers and, though it was often the last thing I wanted to do, I always felt great when it was done and I was able to step into a hot bath.

First choice . . .

It is no good being the kind of person who basks in the sympathy on missing out on a team place, be it for the Curtis Cup or a humble club match.

Certainly, I was never allowed to do that for, if ever I did complain and seek sympathy, my father would point out that I obviously hadn't done enough to be sure of my place. The way he saw it was that you had to be so good that you were not a borderline case but a 100 per cent certainty from the selectors' point of view. His words have come back to me more than once in a Curtis Cup context—notably in 1984 and 1986.

The year 1984 was the only year in which I must confess that I did feel hard done by. I had played in the '82 Curtis Cup and, in that same year, had been chosen for a World cup side of three that finished third in Geneva. Yet when, at the end of the following year, the Ladies Golf Union chose their 12-strong squad from which the '84 Curtis Cup side was to be chosen, my name didn't come into it.

To me it seemed a little unlikely that I could have gone from being in the top three to outwith the top 12 in the space of a year. Rumour had it that they had decided that, at 48, I was just too old. Which was why, when it came to the announcement of the '86 side, I had prepared myself for being rejected again.

I had won the '85 British Women's Stroke-Play at Formby and knew, in my heart of hearts, that if I were to win the Scottish at the start of the following year I would be genuinely worth one of the eight Curtis Cup places. I did win but, at that point, I quite honestly wouldn't have minded too much if they hadn't chosen me. I had met the criteria I had set myself and, still more important, I felt confident that even my father would have said that I had done my bit in making sure I was a certainty rather than a 50/50 case.

Reverting to the 1984 Curtis Cup, there was a deal of adverse publicity when the selectors ultimately came up with their side for Muirfield. Ninety-nine per cent of the golfing public, had they been asked to nominate a team, would have suggested one which took in two or maybe three Scots. Yet the selectors did not choose one; not even Gillian Stewart who was the reigning Scottish champion and had done a lot else besides. There are years when a Scottish champion would not merit inclusion but Gillian was very definitely a player with a bit of class.

The crowds were not bad at Muirfield, but they would have been very much better had there been a Scot. Obviously, all those sitting at home in Scotland and wondering ''Shall we go to the Curtis Cup?'' would have been put off by the fact that they did not know too many of the names in the British team.

Naturally, I had periods of working on my arms, too, having had something of a rude awakening some years ago when David Scott, the professional at Douglas Park, had asked if he could assess the control I had in each arm by watching me hit shots single-handed. I was pathetic with my right hand and not all that good with my left, especially bearing in mind the fact that, as well as having hit so many golf shots, I was actually left-handed. Indeed, the only reason I had not played left-handed in the first place was because there were no left-handed implements available.

I avoided exercises that would have developed my shoulders overmuch and looked, instead, for ones specifically aimed at strengthening that area from the elbow down through the hands. One very good exercise I came upon—and one which might be still more useful to those who never had the same early chance as I did to develop a good basic strength in my arms—is to sit in an easy chair and lay your hand and arm along the arm rest. You then take a weight on a heavy string, or a heavy book, and lift it up and down and up and down, all the time making sure that your arm at the top is at right angles to the chair rest.

Another exercise in which I have great faith is the Henry Cotton tyre routine. The first time I started to bash away with an old club—at the tyre—I was amazed at the lack of resistance, at how everything gave. I thought it a marvellous way of developing strength and speed of hand and, at the same time, I made a point of practising my leg action. You have to do everything you can to stop your legs from getting lazy because, if you have lazy legs, it is a disaster in the golf swing.

After hitting the outside I would then hold the club the other way up and swish the shaft from side to side in the middle of the tyre. In fact, of all the exercises you can do in golf, I can think of none to better that one.

Chapter 4

Practice

Not long after I came back from the 1986 Curtis Cup, I took a sentimental stroll round the practice ground at Dougalston. It's a particularly pretty practice area with its tree-lined surrounds but, at least on that day, I was looking more at the long years of practice I had put in on that little patch of ground. I was unbelievably lucky at Dougalston in that the administrator, Bill McInnes, and the greenkeeper, John Young, allowed me to do much of my work on the course itself. He used to let me hit irons toward the greens and to practise from the bunkers, for there was no practice bunker as such. But that privilege was something I never abused.

If I was hitting full irons, I would always aim them at a stick behind a bunker rather than at the green. Again, I used to make sure that all my work was done at times when I was in no danger of getting in the way of the members. Mostly, I would leave home at about eight in the morning and be back by half past nine, having spent a good half hour on the putting green. Then, when everyone else was on the point of leaving the club at night, I might go out again and put in a further hour.

Much though I loved that practice ground, there were many occasions when I would pretend I was somewhere else. For example, when I had a championship coming up at St Andrews, I would cut out such things as my soft wedge shots. You put them away and they come back later. The main feature of my practice period in these circumstances would have been the run-up shot played with a six or seven iron from 10 to 20 yards short of the green.

My practice bag holds about 60 to 70 balls, although I never expected to come away from a championship with more than 50 in that there is so much traffic in the practice area, with people

27

hitting from all angles. Anyhow, after doing my usual warm-up exercises—a few bends and stretches—I would play a series of gentle half-wedges or nine irons. I would then move on to hit a bag of St Andrews-type pitch-and-runs.

If, on the other hand, I was practising for an event at Sunningdale, I would not be bothering with that last shot at all. Instead, I would be hitting a series of full seven irons, followed by some of the longer irons you are likely to need on that particular course. But, having hit those longer irons, I would always go back to hitting eight or nine irons with a three-quarter swing, mostly for the sake of rhythm.

I never did a lot of practice with my woods. In fact, I went through a spell of leaving them behind altogether in order to force myself to work with my three and four irons, clubs I found relatively difficult.

I know there are those who can work on their swing simply by sitting and thinking about it. I have never been able to do that, although I would plan what I wanted to practise the next day. The usual pointers for me were to take the club away wide on the backswing, to think ''rhythm'' and not to let my legs get lazy. If I didn't remember to take the club away wide, I would sometimes find myself swinging it back round my ankles.

David Scott, the professional at Douglas Park who works with the Dunbartonshire women's team, helped me to combat that tendency by putting two clubs down—one along the line of my feet and another parallel to it on the path my swing should take. Obviously, if I started to swing back too much on the inside, I would hit that second club.

I would happily experiment with the odd Seve Ballesteros tip taken from his strip in the *Sunday Express,* while I also got quite a lot out of instruction books and magazines. I would glance through all the instructional pages and, though there was plenty of material which I did not want to retain, there was almost always some little point worth a try. My favourite book, incidentally, has for some time now been Tom Watson's *Up and Down in Two.*

Towards the end of a practice session I would play a handful of specialist shots, shots such as cut-up wedges or chips from bad lies. Then, maybe, I would set myself a little test of hitting pitches at my golf bag. First, I would be aiming to hit it full toss, then I would try and hit it after a couple of bounces.

If I was at a championship venue and practising by way of warming up before my round, I would head for the practice ground about an hour before I was due off the tee. Ideally, you should be aiming to hit enough shots to get your muscles stretched and to find your rhythm.

I would start off with my usual half wedges or nine irons and would then opt, unfailingly, for a six or seven iron. I always felt at home with a medium iron in this situation in that it's a club which is so easy to hit. One thing you don't want to do before going out for an important game is to whip out your four iron. If you hit a few ropey ones your confidence could be dented.

Can we do it again? Maurice Moir and I set out to defend our Sunningdale Foursomes title. 1961.

Aside from practising well it was important to me not to arrive in a rush. If you are short of time, the kind of relaxed nervousness that can work so well for you out on the course is replaced by a jumpy nervousness which can make it very difficult to think straight. On the same tack, I think practice rounds can help enormously, not just in terms of letting you get to know the course but in allowing you to feel on top, mentally. I would always go out of my way to have a practice round, though there were times when it was simply not possible. On such occasions you could sometimes surprise yourself by doing extraordinarily well without one. However, I think it fair to say that nine times out of ten the lack of a practice round will cost something in the region of two to three shots.

Practice rounds are worthwhile, too, for the middle-handicap players who want, say, to get the best out of an open meeting day. But it is no good setting out aimlessly; you have got to know what you are looking for in the way of bunkers to be avoided and greens where you cannot afford to be over the back.

As for yardages, I always used to take them in the States where you tend to get a uniform bounce of the ball and wind is not often a factor. Over here I was never particularly dependent on them in that there are too many variables. Mind you, I do like to know precise distances when I am within a wedge or nine iron of the green.

Yardages can be particularly useless on a links course and I have lost count of the number of Americans who, having lived with yardage charts all their lives, have found themselves completely thrown on our seaside courses. For myself, I like to have an approximate distance in my head and a good idea of the contour of the ground. Having got that picture, I then rely on feel. In any case, I am not like those professionals who will tell you that they can bank on hitting x number of yards with a six iron or whatever.

Wherever you are, you have to use your head as well as your yardages. For instance, when you are on a tree-lined course, it's no good thinking only in terms of the wind gusting in your face. You've got to look at the very tops of the trees to see what's happening up there. Particularly on the kind of courses we play, a good caddie can be infinitely more valuable than a yardage chart in that he will know that a certain hole might be softer than another, that such and such an apron is way faster than the rest.

Putting

In spite of all the practice I have done over the years, it was only three or four years ago that I learnt how to practise my putting in a way which was constructive.

It was a chance remark from an Irish friend which detonated my sudden attention to this part of my game. "Just imagine," she said, "how good you could be if you were to knock in a couple more putts per round."

I had time on my hands before the start of the 1984 American Amateur championship at Canoe Brook, New Jersey, and, with the practice putting green so good, I decided that this was the ideal opportunity to get down to work. I concentrated on a shorter backswing and on getting pace through the ball. It was the first time that I had ever really applied myself to the mechanics of the stroke.

Team troubles

Difficult team members pop up in teams of every level—from your club third side to your top international outfit.

A good team captain will deal with a troublesome customer from the word go for, if she doesn't, there will come a point when things boil over.

At international level, I should like to see a set procedure where matters of discipline are concerned. The captain should first make it clear to the player that she is not happy about her behaviour. Then, if things do not take a turn for the better, she should give a detailed account of the player's transgressions in the match report that goes into the L.G.U. or whoever. The team member in question should at some point be called upon to give her side of the story. Then, if it is deemed necessary, she should be given a sentence—maybe one to the effect that she will not be considered for any more international teams until the next season.

It would be vital that the player who has served such a sentence should then be held to be on the same footing as everyone else who is aspiring to make teams. All too often in the past we have had situations where a girl feels marked for life once she has been in trouble. She loses heart and the likely corollary will be that the authorities never get as much out of her, in the golfing sense, as they would have done had she been handled correctly.

I kept my putting sharp by doing a lot of putting on the carpet at home. We had a fair-sized hall and, at times when I was waiting for something to cook, I would endeavour to hole a cluster of six- to eight-footers. Anyone can do that and it can make all the difference.

Playing with men

Hector Thomson, my first professional, had based my whole game around my strength and, in order that I should make the most of this power, he encouraged me to play with men. I did this all the time in my early years in Kintyre, while I was not long into golf's mainstream when Dorothea Sommerville and myself had an enormously profitable week playing on a series of different courses in and around Glasgow under the guidance of Eric Brown and his friend Bill Millar. Eric gave us all sorts of little pointers and I remember being more than a little chuffed when, after he had asked me to copy a little chip he had played into the green and I had hit my ball inside his, he said, ''My God, girl, you learn fast!'' At the end of the week he refused to accept a penny for all the help he had given us, making out that the week had done him as much good as it had done us in that he had been able to get his game sharpened for the season ahead.

Some years later, when I was due to captain the 1974 Curtis Cup side in San Francisco, I was delighted when Eric Brown was among those professionals who, thanks to the good offices of Tom Davie of Uniroyal, came to Lanark for a practice match against the girls. I asked Eric that day if, after dinner, he would spend a few minutes talking to the girls about what they might expect when playing against the Americans in the States. He happily agreed and, though what he had to say did not stop his old friend, John Panton, from nodding off, his little speech contained a revelation which made my team sit up. ''Over there,'' he started off by warning them, ''you'll all be nobodies. The press will look only at the Americans.''

The gist of his message was that we shouldn't be frightened and that we should take heart from what he had done when first he went over there. Successful though he had been in these islands no one over there, he said, had given him a second glance. What is more, he had been made to feel still more insignificant when, on going across to the practice ground, he had come up against an impenetrable line of top Americans, none of whom seemed aware of the fact that anyone else might like to hit some shots. Never one to do things by halves, Eric homed in on two of the most celebrated golfers of them all—Ben Hogan and Sam Snead. Then, in a line which would have done justice to any western, he said what he had to say. "Move over boys. I'd like to practise."

Like Eric Brown, I was struck by the difference in American-style practice. In truth, I always used to get excited at going on to a practice ground in America because, at least to me, it was all so incredible. You would see about half a dozen girls with the most outrageous practice routines; not quite standing on their heads but certainly on one leg. They would be there day in, day out, religiously doing what their professionals had advised. And that's only the amateurs I am talking about.

A moment's thought . . .

A moment's thought can be priceless when you are in trouble. If, for instance, you are in long and tangled rough and you miss the shot at the first attempt, stop and ask yourself if it is genuinely within your powers to knock it out or if you wouldn't do better to take a penalty drop.

We are all guilty of acting first and thinking later. In which connection, I was taught a never-to-be-forgotten lesson during the European Women's Team championships in Belgium. I was immediately behind a couple of bushy fir trees and chose to drop two club lengths away under penalty. The moment I had dropped the ball, it came to me that I would have done better to take advantage of the rule that states you can go back as far as you like as long as you keep the trouble between yourself and the hole. I asked the referee if I could start all over again, only to be reminded that once you have taken a drop, the ball is considered to be in play.

One person who made telling use of the "Go-back-as-far-as-you-like" clause was Tom Weiskopf in the year he won the Open at Troon. The American had hit into an impossible position in the whins at the ninth hole. Instead of playing three off the tee, he took a one shot penalty and, keeping the said whins between himself and the green, went right back to the teeing ground at the eighth before making his drop. He then whistled his iron aboard the green and holed the putt for the most improbable of fours. It was a marvellous piece of thinking and one which tells everything about how important it is to know your rules so you can go through the various options in a collected way when you run into trouble.

Never, at any stage of my career, did I do much more than an hour at a time, for I am of the school of thought that it is better to do a relatively short stint rather than a longer period in which you are bound to lose concentration and hit the kind of slack or lazy shot which can be so damaging to the confidence. But, having said that, I knew of several British girls who subscribed to the other view with, among them, England's Ruth Porter. I always used to find out how everyone else did things and, when I asked Ruth how she set about preparing for an event, I was staggered to learn of her routine.

She would start her day by taking a cup of tea up to her parents. Then, having had breakfast, she would get dropped off at the course by her father as he drove into his office. All morning she would practise or play until her father arrived to take her home for lunch. After lunch it would start all over again and she would only pull up having done the equivalent of a full day's work.

I can remember thinking what an incredible amount of golf she was packing into her days. So much more than I was because, at that stage, my golf was still being fitted in around my work rather than vice versa. Though he was good at letting me have days and even weeks off for golf, my father could never have understood my taking that kind of time away from the farm. Looking back, I think it no bad thing in that, when I did get to play, there was always a certain freshness in my game. Nor did I lose that freshness when I moved up to Glasgow for, after my marriage, I had a home and a garden to look after.

Always, in my married life, I tried to keep golf in its place. I was away a lot but when I was at home, I was at home. I would never play on Saturdays and Sundays until I knew when Ian was playing. That way I could arrange to go out at the same time as he did in order that we could have our meals together. I have, incidentally, always loved to cook—something I think I picked up from my mother.

It would be fair to say that I worked hard at my domestic chores and at my golf. That suited me fine, for I don't think I could ever have justified playing on a more full-time basis. Had I been a professional, it would have been different and now, when people ask—as they often do—if I regret not having been born at a time which would have allowed me to play on the WPGA tour, I think my honest answer is "Yes". But it is not so much "Yes" from the monetary side, as from the point of view of wondering if, had I played the game on a professional basis, I could have improved by another two or three strokes.

34

Here you see me, in golfing terms at least, in a thoroughly dangerous position. My club is over the top, across the line. It goes without saying that the shot I hit was not a good one.

This picture pleases me. To my mind, I'm in the perfect position in this instance.

Warming up . . .

The pictures of me warming up are self-explanatory. I can't remember exactly what I did by way of warming up as a youngster but over the last few years I have done more and more in this line. As the muscles begin to lose their elasticity it becomes doubly important to get your body ready for that first tee shot.

I appreciate that the average club golfer would be embarrassed to go through a warm-up routine, even if she did suspect it might be good for her. Yet, if she had been brought up on the Continent, she wouldn't think twice about it in that no one over there would dream of setting out without first doing some bends and stretches and hitting a handful of balls on the practice ground.

The Continentals, like the Americans, are very much more inclined to take lessons than the British—and one of the first things they learn from their professionals is how to start their golfing day. Hector Thomson always used to say to me "Have a few swings to loosen up". I needed them then because I would have been sitting on the bus as I arrived at Machrihanish from school or home.

Where there was a time when I would see a few gentle shots on the practice ground as enough in the way of an introduction to a rigorous work-out, I would nowadays preface those shots by doing some of this swinging from side to side with a club at my back.

What is more, it is these things we are talking about that can make all the difference between a bronze division golfer and a silver division player. For instance, someone who has taken the trouble to warm up as I do—and it doesn't have to look too serious in that you can chat away as you do it—will obviously have a better chance of connecting well with her first tee shot. And no less a player than Jack Nicklaus has said that how you hit your first tee shot is a good pointer to what is going to happen in the rest of the round.

36

Chapter 5

Equipment

The first golf clubs my brother and I got our hands on had hickory shafts. They were given to the family by my mother's cousin and I am afraid we abused them terribly in that we were forever hitting stones around the yard. When, at 15 or 16, I started going to Machrihanish for lessons, I was fortunate enough to use woods that had been made by Hector Thomson himself. He would watch me play with them and, just as he would make adjustments to the way I was hitting the ball, so he would fiddle around with the clubs, shaving a bit off the face to help deter a slice, or maybe altering the loft.

Soon after I had won my first competition away from home—an open meeting at Dunoon—I used my five pounds voucher to buy a couple of Jean Donald woods. These I combined with Bobby Locke irons until such time as I could afford a whole set of Jean Donalds. When I was into my mid-twenties I felt I needed to move on to a full set of men's clubs and I selected Haig Ultras with lightweight shafts. The clubs I carried during the later stages of my championship career were as follows: driver, three wood and five wood; three iron through to nine iron and three wedges.

The reason for the three wedges is that I probably play a bigger variety of wedge shots than most. I have a sharp-bladed implement with a lot of loft, a regular one and a sand wedge. At the time I was working with Elliot Rowan, my wedges went in and out of a vice until they suited me perfectly. In fact, I am today so comfortable with a wedge that, if my life were to depend on hitting one perfect shot, I would see my best chance of survival as a soft wedge hit from around 50 yards.

The one club I would never choose in such circumstances would be my putter, vastly improved though I was in that department towards the end of my career. Somehow, I never achieved the same relationship with my putter as, for instance, did that former English champion and Curtis Cup golfer, Ruth Porter.

The reason I have never had a one or a two iron in my bag is that I have never been particularly happy even with my three, preferring to use my five wood if at all possible. Not too many women are much good with the long irons. JoAnne Carner used to play them well, and probably still does. However, to my mind, no woman has ever been in the same class in this particular area as Catherine Lacoste de Prado, the French amateur who won the American Open. Catherine, whose father won Wimbledon and whose mother was a former winner of the British Women's championship, used to get an incredible height and length with her one iron. But she was immensely strong, with a compact build and muscular swing.

She was also very professional, with a typical incident to illustrate her approach occurring during a European Team championship in Sweden. The set meals we were getting were less than satisfying and it did not take Catherine long to decide that she could not play her best golf on such rations. She called for steaks, insisting that she would take personal responsibility for the costs involved in flying them in, or whatever.

For myself, I would probably not carry anything above a five wood, but I have never been able to understand those who mock seven and eight woods. To my mind, these are wonderful additions to the armoury of those women or older men who are better at sweeping the ball away rather than giving it the kind of hit so necessary to the successful strike of a longer iron. Also, it is worth making the point that there are several top women amateurs now using higher woods—as I found to my cost during the 1986 Vagliano Trophy match in Hamburg.

I was involved in a thrilling match in which Switzerland's Regine Lautens and myself arrived at the 18th, a long and ever-so-slightly dog-leg par four, all square. We both hit good tee shots and it was Regine, one of the most delightful golfers I know, to hit first. I had been debating which iron I would use when suddenly, to my amazement, Regine pulled out a wood and knocked her ball on to the green. I was completely thrown. If she needed a wood, I thought to myself, so must I. I took out my five wood and, for all that something told me to hold it well down the shaft, the ball took one bounce on the green before going over the

40

putting surface. Luckily, it stayed on the uphill slope at the back and I was able to chip back and make the putt to halve the match.

Later, in the locker-room, Regine suggested, mischievously, that she had conned me into playing the wrong club. It turned out that she had used a six wood for her second. She had indeed conned me for, as I admitted, it had never occurred to me that she would have such a club in her bag.

Still on the subject of woods, I never fell for the new breed of metal woods—and that though I spent quite a bit of time experimenting with other people's on two separate visits to the States. However, I was tempted by graphite after I had played against a clubmaker from Wilsons in a match between Troon Ladies and Troon Portland. He had in his locker a graphite-shafted driver he had made himself and he allowed me plenty of time to try it out before I made the big decision to go ahead and buy.

Prepare yourself . . .

Whether you belong to silver division or bronze, preparations for a monthly medal, or whatever, should start long before you tee up at the first. For myself, I clean my shoes and decide what I am going to wear the night before, the idea being to avoid that frenetic business of trying on this and then that directly before I play. On waking in the morning, almost the first thing you do is to look out of the window. And if there's a howling wind and rain your immediate reaction will be one of "Gosh, what a day. What have I let myself in for?" The thing you must never do—and I cannot stress this often enough—is to let that miserable day get to you.

I know, from all my years of competitive play, that it is a bad mistake to arrange to do anything on your way up to the club. Save buying the joint or getting your hair done for the return trip. The last thing you need is to get jumpy because you are worried about being late. That touch of tension and excitement should be stored for your arrival on the first tee.

Try to spend a little time on the practice ground and, having done that, try to make the most of the last few minutes before you tee off, tempting though it might be to chatter to everyone else waiting to get started.

The putting green is the best place to find a bit of peace. Aside from practising your putting, you will be able to gather yourself 100 per cent for an opening drive which, as I have mentioned elsewhere, can to no small extent dictate how you are going to play.

People talk about the extra distance they can get with graphite and I would agree that my driver gave me a great kick in that I picked up a few yards, most of them seeming to come with the bounce of the ball. But, as many of the men professionals find, it is not a club that works all the time. If my swing gets a little quick, the graphite shaft becomes more difficult to control.

I always carry the full complement of 14 clubs and, apart from my wedges, have no particular favourites. If, though, I had to pick out clubs for, say, a five-club event, my choice would be as follows:

three wood,
five iron,
eight iron,
wedge,
putter.

I would always choose the three wood because it is one of those clubs I can do a lot with in terms of going up and down the shaft but, where the irons are concerned, I would make adjustments according to which course I was playing. For example, I would not pick the same selection of irons for Troon Portland as I would for Royal Troon across the road in that at Royal Troon I could happily use my five iron for approaches from 100 yards and under. All of which is the kind of thing everyone should consider before setting out with half a set or, indeed, buying half a set.

When it comes to choosing new clubs, I am influenced greatly by the feeling I get in my hands the first time I pick a club up. That apart, I like to be looking down on a familiar shape of face, just as I always like to be looking down on the same make of ball and would be completely disorientated if, when I went to take a new ball out of my bag, I found a different make had been substituted.

I may be a little set in my ways but I must confess to being horrified when first I picked up a Ping club. But I was made to think again when, on a trip to New Orleans in 1986 to play for the European Seniors versus their American counterparts, I found the former American Curtis Cup golfer, Barbara McIntyre, brandishing a complete set of graphite-shafted Pings. She, of all people, for she had stayed faithful to her old clubs for longer than anyone I have ever known. In fact, I rather think she must have had them from 10 to 15 years.

42

Curtis Cup side 1960. Left to right (back row): Angela Bonallack, myself, Bunty Smith,
Marley Spearman.
(Front row): Philomena Garvey, Ruth Porter, Maureen Garrett, captain, Janette Robertson
and Elizabeth Price.

After recovering from the shock, I could not stop myself from asking what on earth she had been thinking of. She told me that the effect of the new clubs had been nothing short of miraculous. She had been given an extra 30 to 40 yards, together with a new enthusiasm for the game.

If there were two identical sets of clubs lying side by side, I would not simply try out a club from one set and say that those were the ones I wanted to take. I would need to experiment with each club in turn, comparing it carefully with its opposite number from the neighbouring set. It is impossible to explain, but no two clubs feel quite alike. Also, I would be asking the professional to check the swing weights.

Anyone buying clubs for a first time would do better, I feel, to opt for a good second-hand set rather than a relatively cheap new set. But, in buying second-hand clubs, it is vital to have a good professional on hand to advise.

I take a lot of trouble with my clubs, cleaning them after use and changing the grips the moment they have developed a shine which cannot be eliminated by scrubbing. Though at one stage I had a little trouble with my wedding ring rubbing against my finger, I have never had callouses on my hands. This is something I put down to the fact that I have always had good quality grips and top-of-the-range gloves. These, I believe, are two areas in which the aspiring golfer should never skimp. I used a new glove for each event and then demoted it for use on the practice days of my next competition. When it rained, I was always able to dig into my bag and produce an all-weather glove.

Apart from such obvious things as balls and tee-pegs, my check list before a competitive round would take in the following:

towel,
pencils,
markers,
rule book,
roll of plaster,
umbrella,
three or four gloves and one all-weather glove stored in polythene bag,
waterproof trousers.

Where the markers are concerned, I was never happy unless I had with me my favourite marker, one that was hand-made in silver by Hamish Edward, from the well-known family of

Captaining Scotland for the first time. Annette Laing is at the top of the steps above Joan Hastings, Marjorie Fowler and Joan Lawrence. 1966.

Glasgow jewellers. He gave it to me on the occasion of my win in the British Match-Play championship in 1981, inscribing my name, the date, and the championship's initials. It is a precious little gift that has become something of a lucky mascot.

The reason I take my rule book is that no one can hope to stand his or her ground without it. And that applies to everyone, regardless of whether they are playing in a club's third-team match or a full-scale international.

Why, you will no doubt ask, do I only take waterproof trousers? The answer here is that I have never, in 35 years, got used to playing in a waterproof top. I know that they make great claims for the latest designs but, quite frankly, every waterproof jacket I have ever tried makes my swing feel restricted. I would sooner wear several sweaters and get the top layer or so wet.

I have mentioned that I would always opt for top-quality grips and gloves. However, there is one other item on which I would never try to save. Namely, shoes. I prefer a firm leather shoe with a heel rather than a wedge sole. And studs. There are those who ask if I don't find the kind of shoes I wear a little heavy but, if they are good quality and a good fit, the last thing they feel is heavy. I have a dread of going anywhere—be it on the golf course or out in the evening—in shoes that are uncomfortable.

Having forked out for an expensive pair of shoes, I would always take great care of them. My first move, on getting them home, would be to undo all the studs and put a touch of Vaseline in the holes. If you fail to do that, the whole socket can come clean away after the shoes have been worn for a bit.

I would always dry my shoes and clean them at the end of every round and never, repeat never, go out to play in a pair that had not first been whitened or polished. Quite frankly, I could never have played good golf in dirty shoes. I would have been too concerned about them.

Obviously, all the girls have good equipment at Curtis Cup level. But, when one got to America for the 1986 match, there was a distinct difference between the Americans' clubs and our own. Most of the Americans were college golfers who, in the course of their education, study everything there is to know about the game, right down to the latest trends in equipment. It matters to them that they should have clubs bang up to date and, as a result, there is a certain ''sameness'' about their sets. I am not saying that our players' clubs were old-fashioned. Just that there was a far greater variety in terms of makes and shapes.

A little breathing space . . .

Those parents who are anxious to see an offspring progress in golf should appreciate that there comes a moment when the child should be left to stand on her own feet.

Sending a youngster off to play in an event such as the British Girls' championship is like sending her off to boarding school. And, just as in the case of school, parents must desist from interfering, so they should be prepared to give their aspiring golfer some breathing space. It is one thing to watch your daughter's game if you are tucked inconspicuously among a cluster of interested people, quite another to be the only person in hot pursuit of the match.

One parent who always sensed the importance of keeping his distance was Bert Aitken, father of Wilma. When Wilma first started to play in West of Scotland junior events, Bert would help with the organisation. Obviously he was interested in how Wilma was playing and always liked to be kept in touch. However, he would always follow someone else's match rather than hers.

A bad parent is one who talks about his child in front of her, saying something along the lines, ''She's coming along nicely'', or ''We've got our handicap down and we are going to be playing in such and such a thing''. This kind of talk builds resentment and it goes without saying that people will often be rather glad when the girl doesn't do what the proud parent had forecast. All of which is grossly unfair to the child.

Parents should realise that they are not doing their young one any favours by giving her—or him, for that matter—a full and shiny set of clubs. A half set is quite enough at the beginning, while it is better by far that a youngster should be made to work for everything she gets. I was.

There was the time, for instance, when I was helping my father to prepare turnips for a local show. Quick to see the possibilities, I asked him if, in the event of his winning the first prize, I might have the new badminton racket I had wanted for so long. His turnips duly won—and I remember wasting no time in keeping my father to his word.

Parents should not always fix up a youngster's games for her. If the child is keen she will make her own telephone calls and arrangements. Again, when the point comes—and come it will—when he or she is in trouble at the club for looking untidy in the tea-room or playing at the wrong time, do not automatically take the youngster's side. In the longer term, it is much better for her that you should point out that she must accept the rules of the club, whatever she thinks of them.

Finally, the most important thing a parent can teach a child is something I learned from the rally driver, Shiela van Dam. When someone once admired the way she accepted defeat, she told how she always kept a smile on her face "until I get into my own room and shut the door".

Chapter 6

Pressure

It is ballyhoo to say that in the realm of match-play you have to play the course rather than your opponent. I wouldn't actually watch an opponent making her stroke, but I defy anyone not to be aware of the opposition's shot to the flag. You can't help but notice—be influenced.

There have been occasions when I have competed almost better than I know how. For example, I would hole a putt at the 12th or 13th without having realised that it had been for the match. Generally speaking, I'm good at getting myself into a cocoon of concentration, taking a match one hole at a time. However, quite apart from those inevitable days when nothing is going quite right, I have a specific mental weakness in the context of match-play.

Where, in a stroke-play event, I would expect to hole the 12- to 15-footer I needed for a birdie, I cannot, for the life of me, feel the same way about that putt when it comes to match-play and I need it to win the hole. My thinking is along the lines that it is not going to be the end of the world if I don't make it; that I am still going to walk off the green with a half. Again, I could take, say, a six or seven at the 14th hole in a medal round without feeling too depressed, for there is this reassuring feeling that there are holes ahead, each one of which can be seen as a separate entity. In match-play, though, a bad hole late on can seep so much more into your playing of the next hole. You stand on the tee feeling horribly aware of the fact that you are now three down rather than two, or whatever.

Mental handling of a hole is something you learn with experience, albeit sheer ignorance and bravado can get you by when you are a youngster. Most people have a couple of years at the beginning when they know no fear. You arrive on the tee feeling marvellous and you can see your ball sailing over trees or water. There is no small voice inside you saying "I can't do this". I came rollicking down from a 30 handicap to 14 in my first year—but that period of carefree fun is short-lived. As soon as you start winning you create pressures and you find that you spend the rest of your golfing life trying to handle them. Towards the end of my career, I was handling them quite competently, but I regret that I did not come more fully to grips with that side of things much earlier.

Especially at American universities and colleges, today's youngsters are getting a head-start in that direction. They see sports psychologists, while their coaches, too, concentrate much more on the mental considerations. I wish I had had all that but, at the same time, I cannot but suspect that a truly deep-seated confidence is something which cannot appear in a short space of time. Maybe the answer is that you need a combination of the old approach and the new; plenty of straight psychology but an enquiring mind besides. Everyone is different and, for myself, I doubt whether anything could have made up for the discussions I would have with my contemporaries as to what made each of us tick competitively. Discussions such as the ones which would occur every night in the academy of learning that is Gerald Micklem's house on the edge of Sunningdale.

At the time of the Avia and Sunningdale Foursomes, Gerald, a former Walker Cup golfer who has for long been the leading light in the amateur game, would have golfers staying in every room, a typical guest list taking in Michael Burgess and Leonard Crawley; Bridget Jackson, Brigitte Varangot, Angela Ward, Michael Bonallack, Lally Segard, Isa Goldschmid and Janette Robertson. All of them knew what it was to play at international level and they were without doubt the best players of the day in the European amateur arena.

Having listened to everything they had had to say—and the topic was as likely to centre around technique or equipment as the psychology of the game—I would sift through the evening's talk and pick out the little things which I felt might work for me.

Breaking into single figures

Like many another, I became a little stuck when, at 19, I got down to a single-figure handicap. Some people never emerge from that particular tunnel. The potential is there but they are unable to take the next step and to capitalise on what they have.

50

Bound for Mexico City and the World Team championship of 1966. Left to right: Belle Robertson, Ita Butler, Brigitte Varangot, Lally Segard, Catherine Lacoste, Florence Dickson and Ruth Porter.

I have always thought that the reason I managed to work myself clear owed much to my environment. After a spell of tournament play, I would be returning to a part of the world where no one knew enough of women's championship golf to be able to quiz me overmuch on my success or otherwise. The local community would have known all about Henry Cotton and Joyce Wethered but, away from discussions on great players such as these, the golfing talk in our part of the world would have been of such things as the Camel, a most unusual trophy presented by one lady member on her return from India for an annual match between Dunaverty and Machrihanish.

51

Maybe, if I had been missing for a bit, someone would ask, casually, how I had got on but, in the same breath, they would be telling me all about the Young Farmers' dance or noting that it was a dry enough day for haymaking. It was all very different to the kind of scene experienced by the youngsters of today. They play, competitively, almost every week through the summer and are under constant pressure to be seen to be doing great things.

A new dimension was added to my game when, at the age of 23, I was playing in what was only my second major championship, the British Women's Match-Play at The Berkshire. A complete unknown at that level, I played blithely through to the final where I lost to Elizabeth Price. After the match I read press reports discussing why I had chosen to play such a shot when I did. The truth, of course, was that most of the time I wasn't aware of making any choices. I had just stood up and hit. From that moment, I started to think, to weigh up the pros and cons of hitting down one side of the fairway or the other. For instance, on a hole with out of bounds hard on the right, I would be hell bent on taking the safest route.

At the 16th hole on the Old Course, St Andrews, where it is vital not to hit into the Principal's Nose off the tee, I would almost overdo the business of playing safe. In such circumstances, the shot I would hit would not necessarily be well struck. It might look awful but, by hook or by crook, I would get it into the right area. That, after all, is the only thing that really matters.

First-tee nerves

First-tee nerves have gripped me in different ways down the years. Initially, the thought of moving out from the group at the side to tee up my ball filled me with the same kind of nerves that I used to get at school when I was asked to stand up and read out a poem. It was a terror of taking the stage. Latterly, I was not afraid on that score, but there would be a definite catch in my tummy as I wondered if I was going to play as well as I should.

I never thought it a good thing to speak to people in the last few minutes before teeing off. I might say "Good morning" to the starter, but I would then move a couple of steps away in case he or she said something that might be distracting. My next move would be to take a few deep breaths, having first made sure that no one was noticing. After that, I would check my ball and remind myself to swing slowly.

Not far removed from the first tee situation is that which arises out of a long wait. Let us say that things go smoothly until the short fourth or fifth where you arrive on the tee to find three or four couples waiting to hit off. If I had started badly, I would be looking for a bit of encouragement from my caddie at this point. One thing I would not be doing is watching how the others were playing the hole. I would be looking at my golf bag, my feet; anything other than what was happening to those ahead. The last thing I would want to have in my mind's eye would be a picture of someone knocking their ball into sand or thinning it through the back of the green. I would want to be able to tee my ball up ''fresh''.

The game of golf teaches you patience and control but it is in circumstances such as these that it is easy to have a bit of a relapse. I can remember being terribly impressed with the way in which Norman von Nida used to be able to read how different people would react to the assorted pressures of the Open. There were several of us—golfing girls—working on the Open scoreboard one year and each night Norman, who had by then stopped playing and was working for an Australian newspaper, would come and chat to us and, pointing at the board, would say, ''You will be taking that name, that name and that name off the leaderboard tomorrow.''

''How can you tell?'' I asked.

''Well,'' he replied, ''you just get to know the boys who can stay there for the full four rounds, those who have the stomach for it.''

Keeping the emotions in check

During the 1987 match between the seniors of America and Europe, I got round to discussing caddies with Canada's Marlene Streit. Having told me how Jan Stevenson, from the L.P.G.A. tour, has a caddie who does simply everything for her, she made what I think to be a very valid point. Namely, that women need a caddie rather more than men in that they tend to be more emotional.

I have told elsewhere how Tip Anderson refused to entertain the idea of my feeling sorry for myself when I felt a section of the crowd was obviously supporting an opponent. Jan, it seems, is plagued by all sorts of distractions on the course—odd crowd comments, wolf whistles, you name it. Her caddie's main job will be to shield her from such intrusions or, when that isn't possible, to make light of any remarks which might gnaw away at her concentration.

I often wish the selectors in women's golf were as perceptive and as knowledgeable as was Norman von Nida.

I frequently feel irritated and mad at myself on a golf course but I try to contain it, endeavour not to let my outward expressions or my mannerisms convey what I am feeling. Certainly, if I get a lucky bounce off a bunker-top and the ball kicks on to the green I might raise my eyes and join in the crowd's reaction. That would break the tension. However, if I were to miss a three-foot putt, I would never allow myself to slap my side or to convey to my opponent in any way that I was annoyed. If she sees you looking distressed she will feel as if she has won two holes rather than one. Also, if you have reacted badly to that missed putt, your opponent will go on to the next green feeling on top of the world, under the impression that she is the good putter in this match. If, on the other hand, you had reacted not at all to the mishap, she would have gained nothing further from it. For exactly the same reason, I would never, after hitting an indifferent drive or fairway wood, thump my driver on the ground.

Out on the course, I preferred not to talk. I would say "Good shot" to an opponent, but I would never go overboard about one of her strokes. Do that and you are giving her too much in the way of encouragement. What you should be doing, of course, is assuming that every shot your opponent hits is going to be a good one. That way you are not going to be overly alarmed if he or she holes a little chip or a 30-footer.

In times of stress, I always looked to my caddie for support. To me, a good caddie is worth his weight in gold. I started in an era when it was accepted that you needed a caddie and, thankfully, there were a lot of very good ones around. I have always been able to understand how the great players, the Nicklauses and the Watsons, strike up long-lasting relationships with their caddies. The right man can shoulder very much more than merely the bag of clubs. He can take a lot of the pressure.

Tip Anderson, Arnold Palmer's old caddie, was invaluable in terms of helping me with the mental side of things in the Scottish of '85 at St Andrews. I had won a bundle of holes at the start of my final round against Lesley Hope—an Army nurse who had won the championship in 1975 at Elie and been runner-up to Gillian Stewart in 1979 at Gullane—but, after 11 holes, I had been brought back to square. Then, at the 12th, Lesley had the chance of taking the lead for the first time. When she holed her eight-footer, there was some exuberant clapping from players in her age-group standing to the side of the green. When I proceeded to match her par, by making my six- or seven-footer, there was only a polite ripple of applause. I remarked to Tip that it was pretty obvious whom the gallery wanted to win. He sprang back at me at once. ''To hell with the gallery,'' he said. ''Who needs a gallery, anyway?'' What he had done was to nip my ''sorry for myself'' feelings in the bud.

At the very next hole I was rewarded for all the practice I had put in at Dougalston in the months before. My little pitch-and-run, from a somewhat uninviting lie, finished no more than a foot from the hole. I went one up and ultimately won at the 16th.

Patricia Davies, sister of Maureen Garner, a former Curtis

A winning Dunbartonshire County side.

Cup colleague, is another "caddie" with whom I achieved that perfect bond that can exist between caddie and player. She was working for me at Conway when I won my first British Match-Play championship. I was playing in the final against Wilma Aitken, a fellow member of the Scottish team and a good friend. It was an unreal situation in that we were staying together and, on the night before our match, the couple who owned the house had gone out, leaving us on our own. Wilma rang home to tell her boyfriend she was in the final and it was eventually agreed that he and Ian should drive down from Scotland together to watch us.

My thoughts that night were not along the lines "I must beat Wilma". All I was telling myself was that I had to play well. Early on, I did just that and, leaving the 12th, in weather conditions fouler than any I have ever known, was six up with six to play. It was on the next tee—and it was most unlike me—that I made some kind of joke to Patricia about the shot I planned to play under the wind. The hole in question was a short one and, in the circumstances, I should have been looking for a bread and butter shot. Where I went wrong was to be far too ambitious. I sliced the ball, leaving myself as much as 50 yards short and wide of the green. I lost that hole and each of the next five.

My overridding feeling as I left the 18th green all square was one of acute embarrassment. There was a 100-yards walk between the 18th and the first tee and, as we made our way down the path, Patricia told me to clear my mind of all thoughts, to think I was back at the beginning, playing my first hole of my first round.

It was sound psychology, although I did allow myself a short exchange with one of Ian's friends, a former Rangers player. I myself am an avid Celtic supporter and there had always been a lot of banter between the two of us, with my referring to Rangers' lucky penalties. I can remember remarking, "I could do with one of those Rangers penalties now."

"Not a bit of it," he answered, reassuringly.

I holed what was a tremendous pressure putt—a five-footer—for a half at the first and we moved on to the second, a par three. Wilma hit her ball just through the green, my mental impression at the time being that she was heading for a three rather than a two. I took a six iron and, just as I was about to start my swing, I stopped. Turning to Patricia, I said that I didn't think I had the right club.

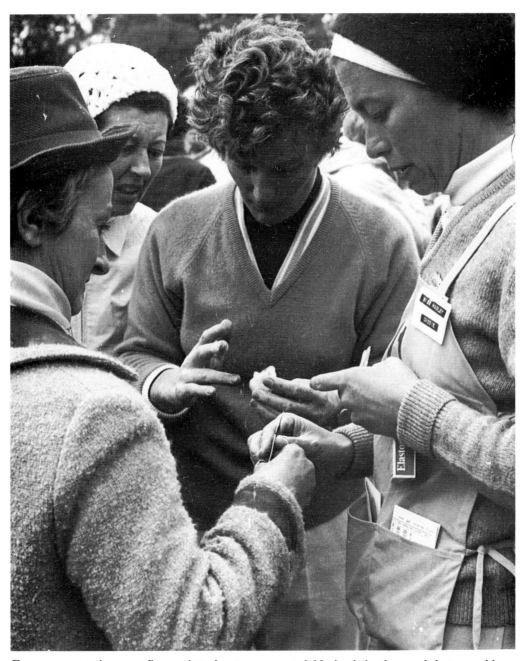

Emergency repairs on a finger ripped not on some prickly bush in the rough but, would you believe it, on the inside of the hole.
World Team championship, Melbourne. 1968.

"Where do you want to hit it?" she queried. "Into the trouble over the back? Take it from me, you've got the right club."

I took her word for it and came up with one of those shots that are down the flag all the way. It finished within 12 feet of the hole. Wilma played a choppy shot to five feet and I then proceeded to putt dead.

As I was standing by, waiting for Wilma to tackle her five-footer, Patricia turned to me and said, "What are you thinking about? You should have your mind on how you're going to play the next hole." She was one hundred per cent right. I did as she said but, out of the corner of my eye, I saw Wilma's putt miss.

It was only after that match that I realised the full extent of the agonies a caddie must endure. Patricia had taken an awful responsibility upon herself by insisting that I use that six iron. Just imagine how she would have felt had the ball gone through.

Someone met me with a whisky as I arrived back at the clubhouse. It may be a terrible thing for a Scot to say, but I don't particularly like whisky. However, I had hardly begun to make my apologies when Patricia made it clear that if I didn't need it, she did. I took a look at her face and she was completely drained.

In retrospect, that was possibly the most crucial match of my career in that, had I finished on the losing side, I don't think I would ever have played competitively again. It may only have been 1981 but people were already telling me that I was too old to win any more major championships and, quite frankly, I had begun to believe them.

People often ask if there was a cumulative pressure attached to winning something like the Scottish for a sixth and a seventh time. Quite honestly, the answer—at least for me—was no in that I was never particularly interested in setting records of that kind. There were occasions when I won the Scottish twice in a row and then, for some reason or another, did not enter it the following Spring. Some of my friends simply couldn't understand how I hadn't wanted to make it three in a row. In fact, keen though I always was to win any championship at the time I was playing in it, I have never been able to give an accurate run-down on my record.

On the subject of learning how to win, I had some of my finest lessons from golfers such as Bunty Smith and Marley Harris. They taught me that you win from inside your head. What is more, I soon realised that it wasn't just on the course that you could pick up little gems in terms of insight into what made them the great players they were. Quite often they would let slip the odd clue over a cup of tea.

For all that, it was in mid-round that I had a memorable tip from Bunty. We were playing in the Avia Foursomes over the Blue Course at The Berkshire and she hit a particularly fine iron just a few yards away from a flag tucked behind a yawning sand trap. I was quick to compliment her on what I felt had been a truly marvellous shot, adding that it must have been doubly difficult with the bunker right in front. She took me on one side and explained, gently, that the bunker hadn't come into it at all. ''I was aiming 12 feet left of the hole and, in using that line, I had no bunker in front of me.''

Scottish Sportsman and Sportswoman of 1968. Jackie Stewart and myself.

Marley had a wealth of information to impart for, having taken to the game late, she had used her head all the way. But maybe nothing that she said or did helped me more than a remark she made after we had played each other in the Home Internationals. We had had a great game in which she beat me at the 16th or 17th. As we walked back to the clubhouse she was generous enough to say, "You made it hard for me today". In other words, she had conveyed to me—at a time when I was still painfully shy and unsure of myself—that she thought I could play a bit. It did great things for my confidence.

In addition to being able to work so well with a caddie—and my old primary school friend, John McMillan, deserves a mention in this capacity for the many times he took a week away from Campbeltown to help me out—I always had another great plus which does not seem to have been given to very many. Namely, that I was mostly able to forget any worries as I shut the front door. Mind you, on an important day, my preparation would by then already have begun.

Before the off

I have always had this tremendous excitement before a match; an excitement that would hit me even in the hours leading up to so seemingly mundane an affair as the monthly medal. In my youngest golfing days, even the prospect of a match between Dunaverty and Machrihanish—an evening fixture—would have me feeling this way. My appetite would disappear and, instead of the usual meal everyone would have after milking, I would opt for a piece or two of my mother's home-made oatcakes. (She made the most marvellous oatcakes which were dried on an old-fashioned rack in front of the fire just to get that extra curl on them.)

I rather think that every competitor has something of this feeling and if it is not there you know that something is wrong. You would not want to interrupt it. A rushed morning could ruin things, as could a bad piece of news. Nor would it do if you were to get too keyed up—something which can happen if someone has irritated you that morning.

In 1986, I had it exactly right both before the Scottish championship at St Andrews and the Curtis Cup.

Receiving the New Zealand Women's Match-Play trophy from Lady Porritt, wife of the Governor-General. 1971.

Accentuate the positive . . .

I have known plenty of golfers who, if they play the first hole well, take it as a bad sign, believing that a lousy finish is almost certainly on the cards. That type of negative thinking will inevitably affect a score. And it won't be for the better.

For the Scottish, I travelled each morning from Broughty Ferry with my brother-in-law. He is Polish by birth and a chess player who nowadays competes on a local level but at one time competed nationally. On that journey, he knew not to talk too much. A competitor himself, he understood that my preparation for the match ahead was already underway.

For the Curtis Cup, I was each morning at a high pitch, but I wasn't barking at my caddie, nor was I irritated by anyone else. We had this drink which had to be made ready—a drink crammed full of vitamins—and before each match we had to prepare it by getting a measure of the powder into a bottle with a smallish neck. How you handled this operation was in itself a pointer to how you were going to cope. To my great relief, I found myself doing it all without getting even mildly flustered.

I used to be fascinated by stories of how others felt in their preparation. Bobby Locke, for example, would never carry a holdall or even dream of lifting his golf clubs out of his car. Simply because he did not want to have that sort of weight in his hands before he had to tackle such delicate things as putts.

Bunty Smith once told me that she found it doubly difficult to hit the right note when Roy Smith, the man she was to marry, first came to watch. Having him there added an extra dimension to the day's pressures: it was at once inspiring but something new with which she had to cope. Bunty also averred that she knew when she was going to play well. I remember her describing this ''certain thinness, a sense of delicacy in my hands''. When she had that, her short game was usually very good. I knew what she meant because I can get that same feeling, too.

Before I went out to play, I was very careful not to do any heavy jobs. I would never, for example, dig the garden or do anything else in the garden without wearing gloves. I would like to have my hands and fingers as perfect as possible. By that I mean they would have to be perfectly groomed, with my nails short and well prepared. If they weren't, I couldn't get that lovely sense of touch and softness. Even the peeling of vegetables could take away from that feeling. All of which goes to show how many ordinary and often unconsidered things can have a bearing on your play.

The kind of high you get from winning a match can stay with you for days and, likewise, the disappointment you feel at a loss is apt to linger. And that is something which takes me back to an early lesson I had from my father.

In the summer the highlight of the week was our foursomes

Curtis Cup ''possibles'' enjoying a day at Lanark with Scotland's leading professionals. 1974.

John Panton, myself and the late Ronnie Shade.

match against the visitors. I always played but there came a day when, having hit the ball downright badly at the weekend, I decided that I would not participate. My father was musing on whom I might get as my partner when I told him I would not be playing.

"Why not?" he asked.

"Because I'm playing so badly," I replied.

There was a silence, as there always was, with my father. But, when he did eventually say something, one listened. "Well," he continued, "If you don't think you should be playing in the foursomes this week, just because you are not playing well, I think you should be asking yourself if you should ever play in the foursomes again."

He went on to say that I was looking at things in a very selfish way, only wanting to play when I was playing well. He advised me to ring up and put in an entry and, as you will have guessed, I did not need to be told twice.

Ironically, it so happened that I played well on the day and was in a winning partnership. I went on to learn that there were plenty of days when you would go into a match without feeling perfectly poised. And on those occasions you just had to do your best to salvage the situation.

Certainly, that was the position in which I found myself when I was back at Machrihanish in 1966, trying to defend the Scottish title I had won for a first time at Nairn. I was desperate to do well in front of my family and friends. My brother, for example, had never seen me playing in a championship. But, in staying back at my mother's, I was never "thinking golf" in the way I would have had I been in a boarding house with a couple of my fellow competitors.

Although I went on to win the championship, I had to come back from the dead—two down with five to play—against Joan Rennie in the semi-final. It was a desperate match, one fraught with distractions. A local, who had had rather too much to drink, hailed me like a long-lost friend as we were playing down the ninth. Nowadays, I would have managed to extricate myself from such a situation but, at that stage of my career, I was fearful of sounding unpleasant and had to get the caddie to quieten the chap for me.

Another little memory which illustrates just how fragile was my concentration that day was of what happened at the 12th. I had hit a strong three iron and, in the course of it, taken quite a divot.

There were a couple of farmers watching, neither of whom had ever seen a championship final before. They studied the divot at length and, just when I felt they must comment on what had, after all, been a darned good shot, one turned to the other and remarked, ''This wid be fine ground for growin' potatoes.''

Bunkered . . .

One of the secrets of bunker play is to know your bunker method and to have it in your head as you walk into the trap. If you do not have any kind of escape formula in your head you will never get out.

Should the bunker have a particularly high face, or the lie be a bad one, the higher handicap golfer must ask herself if she wouldn't be wiser to hit out sideways and waste one shot rather than three.

If, at the first attempt, you leave the ball in the sand, don't rush up and give it another whack. The thing to do is to turn your back on the ball and to walk out of the trap.

You will be annoyed and embarrassed but, by stepping out of the bunker for a few seconds, you will be able to compose yourself.

Good technique is all-important and it is worth taking lessons on bunker play and practising to the point where you no longer think in terms of a bunker as something to dread.

Using the driver . . .

Looking at the first picture, I am satisfied that I am in a good, relaxed address position. The basics, as I have said so many times, are all-important and if you are wrong at the address there is little chance of things coming right thereafter. As with starting a car, I like the feeling of beginning slowly and smoothly, going up one gear at a time.

In picture number two I am in a good neutral position, not having let the club cross over at the top—an occasional fault of mine the camera has captured on page 35. What I have done right in this swing is to take the club away nice and wide, thereby avoiding that tendency to get over the top. I have clung on firmly to the club with the last three fingers of my left hand and I look well balanced. Transferring my weight correctly is something I have always found relatively easy, though if I am tired or maybe out of practice, my legs and feet are apt to be a bit slow. My position through the ball is good with my legs working fast and driving forward. As you get older, you have to remind your body to do the things which you maybe did not have to think about when you were younger. For me, my main thoughts, latterly, were "rhythm" and "fast legs".

In reference to my follow-through, Hector Thomson always used to tell me that my swing had to look right at the end, that I had to finish in a well-balanced position. "Look good for the camera," he would say. What he meant by this was that if you strove for a well-balanced finish, what had gone before would most likely be similarly under control.

In order to firm up my finish and my swing in general, I would often go out and swish the clubhead through thick grass. That made me hold on to the club and, once I could get Hector's "good position for the camera" at the end of one of those swings, I knew that my whole action was becoming more solid.

I am not, of course, saying that mine is a swing anyone will necessarily want to copy. However, with my results down the years suggesting that I must do quite a bit right, I think it is perhaps worth giving you an insight into my shotmaking and how I feel about it.

Chapter 7

Good Basics

Golf is a difficult game but by no means as difficult as the manifold books and magazine articles on instruction would suggest. I myself have read all the books from cover to cover and, though I have taken a lot from Tom Watson's *Up and Down in Two* and quite a bit from other sources in terms of little tips, I long ago satisfied myself that nothing matters more than having good basics. If you adopt the perfect grip and align yourself correctly, technically at least you cannot go too far wrong.

But, of course, good technique in itself does not make a champion, even if you add to it endless hours of hard work. The two can make you into a better golfer but not better beyond a certain point. The few who succeed in crossing the divide are those who have learned to educate their minds to work correctly amid the pressure of tournament golf.

Bernhard Langer is a fine example of what I am saying. He was at one stage riled because of his shakiness over the shorter putts, but he had the strength of character to win that particular battle. Tom Weiskopf had a wonderful method but did not have what it takes, mentally, to make the best of it. Had he had Gary Player's head he would have been some player but, as Lee Trevino is fond of reiterating, God never gave anyone everything. I think he mentioned Arnold Palmer as having no great flair from sand, while Trevino felt that he himself had been given none too generous a helping of length.

What he went on to say was that God offers everyone a challenge—and that is something with which I agree whole-heartedly. The most important thing I had to overcome was an inferiority complex. Because of my shyness, I went through a phase of thinking that people who were sophisticated had something over me.

Also, like many another, I had to learn to keep a hold on the nerves that are, after all, coursing through your body at all times. I seldom felt them on the tee, for the tee-shot to me is the most natural shot in the world and there is no time to be thinking of the things that can go wrong. It was in doing a scaled-down version of the real thing, the half shots, the short approaches and the putts, that the doubts would be inclined to surface.

So much control is needed for the little shots and, for myself, I ultimately found that the easiest way to acquire it was by picking a set target on the practice ground and concentrating, on my first few balls, on finding precisely the correct length of backswing. Too short and the shot would be a hard, inelegant dunt; too long and I would find myself automatically decelerating at impact.

Having married the length of swing to the distance, I would then concentrate on it throughout the practice session and only leave for home once I had committed it firmly to my mind. Countless such sessions meant that when it came to being faced with, say, a 40-yard approach in a championship, I would think back to a similar length of shot I had been practising and be able to play the ball more or less from memory.

Returning to the basics, it really hurts me to see a youngster with a bad grip for, having been around in this game for so many years, I know exactly how limiting a bad grip can be. Judy Rankin did, it is true, get to be the number one of the women's professional game in the States with a most outrageous left-hand position on the club. However, I think it fair to say that she got where she got despite rather than because of her grip. Also, while she did get to the top spot, she did not stay there in the way that Jack Nicklaus stayed at the top. Maybe, in her case, she left it too late to effect a change. She was lucky to get away with it for, to most people, such a grip would have spelt disaster. Which is why, when I see a player whom I know to be having lessons being allowed to play on with a bad grip, I make a mental note that the professional she is going to cannot be very good.

Moving on from the grip, the backswing and the through swing are often broken down in instructional material into a host of different parts. Here, again, I feel the authors are simply making the game out to be ten times more difficult than is necessary, for the only thing a player really needs to think about is making a natural turn away from the ball and a natural turn back into it.

If you look at a line of top professionals—men or women—on the practice ground, you will find that no two players are swinging alike. Among the women, you might see JoAnne Carner hitting the ball for all she is worth and, then, a little further along the line, the gently swaying swing of Chako Higuchi.

I have not got the most attractive swing in the world, but it does have the merit of being natural. My abiding sin is that instead of standing there and making a turn, I am apt to move back away from the ball. I can play the game successfully enough like this, but there has always been the odd period—maybe precipitated by a bad result—when this movement or sway can get me into trouble. In moving out of a secure turn I get a little lost.

The legendary Cecil Leitch, in front of her beloved Silloth, presenting me with the British Stroke-Play Trophy in 1972.

It was a tendency I picked up during my first four or five years of married life when I didn't have much time for golf tuition. Instead of following up the excellent start I had been given by Hector Thomson, I would look for guidance from instructional strips in the Sunday papers or from books. I seized upon one craze after another. One moment I was trying to keep my right elbow tucked rigidly into my side—a theory completely disproved by Jack Nicklaus—and the next I was striving for an artificially one-piece backswing.

However, the thing which started a slice which stuck with me throughout the early '60s was a sudden fad—on whose part I cannot remember—for playing everything off the left foot. Not knowing then what I know now about the importance of alignment, I got myself in a real muddle and, by the time I went to Elliot Rowan for help, the ball was actually outside my left foot.

I learnt from Elliot and, indeed, from all the American women professionals I would watch, the importance of laying a club along the ground during my practice stints and checking and re-checking that I was aiming on target with the ball in the right position.

Where, in those early years, I had trouble with that slice, my bad shot towards the end of my career was one which would dive straight left. I would get to the top of my swing and then, by moving my shoulders over and round, hit the ball with something akin to a chopping motion. It was not a hook, but every bit as damaging.

Still dealing with the more unsavoury shots, I was lucky enough never to suffer from a case of "the yips". I missed my share of short putts but never had days when I was taking 40 or 41 putts. A bad day for me was 36 putts, although I was uncomfortably aware of the fact that Bunty Smith used to insist that a top-class amateur should be taking no more than 31 or 32 putts on a bad day and that she should be aiming at an average of 28 or 29 putts. I always used to think that she was being a little too ambitious until I studied the statistics emanating from the women's professional tour in the States. Out there, in recent years, girls have been topping the lists in terms of putting averages with 24 or 25 putts per round.

As well as being spared "the yips", I thankfully never really knew what it was to shank. I did do one once during the practice days for the Home Internationals at Porthcawl but, luckily, there were mitigating circumstances. I had had to hit the ball from around waist height and, when the girls began to rib me, mercilessly, Marjorie Draper, or Marjorie Peel, as she was then, sprang to my defence and said that anyone could have shanked from such a position and that they should reserve their laughs for the real thing.

The only shank with which, so to speak, I ever got involved was that belonging to my brother-in-law. From that admittedly limited experience, I concluded that the shot came from having the ball in the wrong place at the address and rolling the clubface open. In which connection it must be said that the smooth, easy swing is much more likely to survive moments of high tension than one which is jerky and bitty.

I often used to think how nice it would have been to be like Bjorn Borg and have a Leonard Berglin at hand to keep a constant look-out for the little things that can go wrong and catch them before they develop into anything major. However, coaching is expensive and, in the amateur game, not too many can afford anything more than a few check-ups dotted through the season. It is for this reason, I have deduced, that I used to become so attached to my caddies. They were not able to advise on technique, but the sense of security I would get from having a good caddy on my side was, at least to me, worth very much more than the fee.

Chapter 8

'Sixties and 'Seventies

Having reached the final of the British Match-Play championship in 1959 and having shown the selectors that I had not "lost it" when Maurice Moir and I won the Sunningdale Foursomes the following Spring, I was duly chosen for the 1960 Curtis Cup of that year at Lindrick.

I had no real idea of what awaited me; no notion of what it would be like playing in front of crowds in excess of 14,000. Back in Southend there was no such thing as a stranger, let alone 14,000 of them. On a trip to Campbeltown you would seldom see anyone who could not be placed by you or one of your companions. They were familiar faces, all, even if you could not actually put names to them.

However, my first memory of Lindrick is not so much of the crowds and the match itself as of a night during the preliminaries when fire broke out in the hotel. You always wonder what everyone will save at such a time and I can still picture Janette Robertson running downstairs, clutching her jewellery and wearing her international blazer over her nightdress.

Again, I remember the ubiquitous Dai Rees rushing around in the days leading up to the match. He was not our coach as such but, with his experience of playing against the Americans, he was excellent value in terms of helping to give us the necessary belief.

I have written on another page of the fear I used to have of taking the stage, of drawing attention to myself in any way. It was a problem I had started to overcome but, alas, I was not ready for that first elevated tee they have at Lindrick. Ruth Porter won her single and we mustered a further 1½ points in losing 6½–2½. It was an awful hammering and, for my own part, I must confess to having been totally overawed. I had been frightened and self-conscious and such feelings had been reflected in my golf.

75

If I was never fully to forget that introduction to the Curtis Cup scene, I was yet able to sweep it to the back of my mind with my impending marriage. Ian and I were married in St Blaans by the Reverend James Marks, the successor to ''Old Mac'', of whom I have talked in an early chapter. Janette Robertson was married at much the same time—to a former Scottish internationalist in Innes Wright—and, with the two of us being paired together for the Home Internationals of that year at Gullane, it goes with out saying that everyone was asking, ''How are the two brides doing?''

Though I enjoyed that period of early married life when I was making new friends in the Glasgow area, there is no denying that my golf began to suffer as the regular ''polishing'' sessions I had had from Hector Thomson back at Machrihanish become more and more occasional. Added to the fact that I was so far away from my old mentor, there was the further complication that he was getting on in years. But there was one lesson of a kind I had from him—and he was by then as much as 92—that I have never forgotten. Golf had just become popular on television and, when I went to call on Hector on one of my trips home, he had just been watching the Open.

''Belle,'' he announced, ''you have got to work harder on your putting. These players I have been watching might miss one putt under six foot over four rounds but they're not missing any more.''

He was quite right, and what he said sank in more and more over the years, the only reason it didn't have even more effect being that it was not until the early '80s that I finally sorted out my putting technique.

No doubt because of the lack of regular check-ups, my progress slowed but, as runner-up in the Scottish championship of 1963 as, indeed, I had been in 1959, I was chosen to represent Scotland in the World Cup of 1964 at St Germain. (At that point, the home countries entered separately.) I had never been abroad before and, in purchasing my passport, opted for one of those three months holiday ones you could buy at that time. When the captain asked me why I had not got the same long-term edition as everyone else, I explained how it had occurred to me that I might never need a passport again.

The World Cup, of course, was a tournament which took you to all corners of the golfing globe. In 1966, for example, we went to New Mexico on the very eve of the Olympics and it was there that I set what was a World Cup record by returning a 69. Two years later and we were in Australia, having travelled out via India. For me, a lingering memory of that trip was of a journey from the airport in India on which we saw a dead man lying on the roadside. The driver went round him and, no doubt thinking he was putting our minds at rest, explained how the dustcart or its equivalent would be picking up the body before too long.

Returning to golf at home, it was not until 1965—at Nairn—that I won my national title for the first time. I was 29 by then. Quite old!

Long though it had taken and many though the disappointments had been along the way, it meant much to me that my father was still alive at the time. He had not been the same man since breaking his femur in a fall on an icy road and I can see him

Receiving the Babe Zaharias Trophy from the late Charlotte Beddows, a former Scottish Champion who was still playing good golf in her 80s.

now, leaning on his walking stick on our top step, as I drove up to the family home on the Monday after the championship. I had been wondering for much of the journey what he would say and now the moment arrived.

"Well!" he began, "you've managed it at last."

Before the end of the year he was dead.

In 1966, for the first time since that debacle at Lindrick, I was back in the Curtis Cup, the match being played at Hot Springs, Virginia. This was another annihilation for the British side and, though I managed to salvage two half points, one from my singles with Anne Welts, I was again bitterly disillusioned.

We stayed on for the American Amateur at Pittsburgh where they had the longest final in the history of the event, an amazing match in which JoAnne Carner defeated Marleine Streit at the 41st hole.

Barbara McIntyre, of Curtis Cup fame, had been joined that week by the legendary Scottish teaching professional, Bobby Cruikshank. He had volunteered that I was a wonderful iron player and I was grateful for what he said. However, I knew, in my heart of hearts, that I was nowhere near as good as I should be, that my golf was horribly stuck. In fact, I toyed with the idea of giving up for, even at that juncture, I had had quite a good innings.

Almost the very day that I arrived back in Scotland, Ian and I moved into our house in Buchanan Drive, a Bearsden address at which we stayed for 21 years before moving, in 1986, into a flat just a mile or so away.

At much the same time as we went to Buchanan Drive, an old friend of Ian's, Elliot Rowan, became the professional at Douglas Park, a club just round the corner. Elliot took an interest in my golf and it was during one of our games together—at the fourth hole to be precise—that he spoke out on the subject of the slice that had begun to seep into my play. Having stood silently by as I hit yet another ball left to right, he came across and lined me up correctly for, as I was later to realise, I had been facing way left of target and coming across the ball.

"Now," he instructed, "hit it from there."

I said to myself "This man is silly" and decided I would show him just how far into the field I could hit from this new position. As you will have guessed, the ensuing shot flew maddeningly straight and served to convince me that I needed Elliot's help.

I did not play competitively in 1967 but instead worked solidly

78

at getting my technique as correct as it had been in those days when I used to go to Hector Thomson. Only this time, being that bit older, I asked questions and generally got to understand the ins and outs of my swing.

Whenever Elliot had a spare half hour, he would give the house a ring and I would go dashing down to the club. I worked like that for a year and, at the end of that spell, all the effort began to pay dividends in that my golf was probably the best it has ever been on my return to the competitive scene.

Over the next few years I played in Curtis Cups, World Team championships—and, indeed, everything there was to play in. Where the championships were concerned, I won the British Women's Stroke-Play and the Scottish in each of 1970 and 1971, while I also won the New Zealand championship of 1971, not to mention the Daks Woman Golfer of the Year award and my second Scottish Sportswoman of the Year title.

Frank Moran Trophy Presentation, 1972
(Left to right): Mrs Belle Robertson, Mr Frank Moran, Mr W. S. McIntosh Reid (Judge),
Mr Eric B. Mackay, Mr Wm. Kemp, Mr Norman Mair, Mr Alastair M. Dunnett
(Judge), Lord Clyde (Judge), Sir James W. McKay (Judge).

It's a terrible thing to have to confess but though, for a time, I had the feeling that all this could go on for ever, my enthusiasm all of a sudden evaporated. There was a dreariness instead of a freshness about the prospect of a game of golf and even the most exotic of golfing trips no longer held out any appeal.

I needed a breathing space, although I was happy enough to be asked to act as non-playing captain of the Curtis Cup in both 1974 and 1976. In fact, I was the first to receive this double honour. We lost 5–13 in San Francisco in 1974 and 6½–11½ at Royal Lytham and St Annes two years later. The results were more disappointing than disastrous, for the Americans were particularly strong at that time, with Nancy Lopez making her one and only appearance in the match in 1976.

In my role as captain I had to play practice rounds alongside such as Maureen Walker and Suzanne Cadden and, in helping them, I found my own enthusiasm beginning to resurface. It helped, too, that as I stood on the sidelines watching those two Curtis Cups, I was struck by the notion that I was a rather better player than ever I had believed. Such thoughts, coupled with the fact that I didn't like the idea of gradually losing touch with the many good golfing friends I had made around the world, had me accepting an invitation to play in the 1978 American Amateur championship at Sunnybrook.

Since I felt a little awkward about the prospect of teeing up in this major event without having had anything in the way of competitive practice, I decided to use the Scottish championship at Prestwick as a warm-up. As luck would have it, I managed to win, beating Joan Smith by two holes in the final. That done, I went on to lead the qualifiers at Sunnybrook, finishing ahead of the American and British Curtis Cup golfers who had gone on to the championship after the match at Apawamis.

Inevitably, there were those who said I should have been in that British team but, though there was an occasion—mentioned elsewhere—when I did feel sore about being left out of the side, that was not it. My results had come too late for the purposes of the 1978 instalment. From Sunnybrook I went home to win all my singles in the home internationals of that year at Moortown. All of which had me well and truly back on the bandwagon.

An Investiture at Holyrood, July 10, 1973.

Royal perks . . .

I was fascinated when Princess Anne became engaged to Mark Phillips, for Mark Phillips was the quiet young man I had been speaking to at a luncheon at the Guildhall at which the Princess was the guest of honour. There had been no talk of any romance at that time and I am afraid I did not think to be even vaguely suspicious when he supplied the answer to a remark I made about the Princess being thinner than I had expected—namely, that she had been in hospital for a spell.

Another exchange which comes back to me from that day was one involving Dinah Henson, who had just been out to New Zealand on the same Commonwealth team as myself, and the Princess. When the latter had remarked on the very different ages of the team members, Dinah, who never normally said anything, suddenly volunteered, "I suppose you were thinking we'd all be old ladies dressed in tweeds".

"I'm afraid I was," returned the Princess.

It was way back in 1964, at St Germain, that the Duke of Windsor took a lively interest in the performance of the British players in the World Cup. The Duke was a member of the club and, as such, felt constrained to apologise for the crowd's lack of courtesy towards the Irish girl who had been playing alongside Catherine Lacoste and Barbara Fay Boddie. The spectators had, he said, been disconcertingly restless.

The following day he noted that Ireland and Scotland had both improved on their first round performances and asked if he might join us at our tea table. When making the order, the Duke handed a small silver box to the waiter. Noting our curiosity, he explained how he always carried his own special brand of tea.

After someone had mentioned the Duchess by asking if she played golf, which she did not, the Duke went on to say that he was terrified of going home that night. His wife, he explained, had a passion for shoes and he was frightened that he might have 10 or 12 pairs to pay for on his return.

There was an American Curtis Cup—that at San Francisco in 1974—when Ronald Reagan had goodwill messages for both teams while, back at home, the 1976 sides were asked to Buckingham Palace. As we arrived, there was an artist with a battered Renault in the inner courtyard who was clearing up after a morning session of painting the Queen astride her horse.

The Hon. Lady Mary Morrison, a lady-in-waiting, was among those to greet us and we were told to do a mini-curtsey rather than the real thing. We were going to have coffee with the Queen and, hating coffee as I do, I had to instruct Suzanne Cadden to drink hers quickly in order that we could then swop cups.

We had been encouraged to make conversation with Her Majesty and, after introducing my team, I asked the Queen if she had ever tried golf.

"Yes," she said, "but the clubs were too heavy. I felt a little awkward with them."

She went on to talk of her father's enthusiasm for the game and mentioned the course at Balmoral. Also, she spoke of a recent trip to Japan in which she had been fascinated to see the Japanese hitting balls from their multi-storey driving ranges.

When I went along with Ian and my mother to pick up my M.B.E. at Holyrood, it was all a little technical from the point of view of the presentation. I had to remember to walk six paces forward, turn left and take two further paces forward before having the medal pinned on—and there were similarly complex instructions for the return journey.

I was lucky in that I was among the few people the Queen spoke to that day.

"Are you," she asked, "the lady who plays golf?"

She enquired as to whether I was about to play in anything of note and, when I told how I was just off to Buenos Aires for the World Team championships, she wished me the best of luck after having mentioned—very interestingly, I thought—that it must be fascinating for me to travel to so many different parts of the world.

There was nothing going on after the ceremony at Holyrood—all of which was a bit of an anticlimax as against what had happened at Buckingham Palace in 1972.

After the aforementioned Hon. Lady Mary Morrison had sought me out and said, "I hope to see you in Islay some day", we were given permission to watch the changing of the guard from inside the courtyard. Having always been under the impression that the guards never spoke, we could hardly believe our ears when one of those coming on duty said to one of those leaving, "Anything happen this morning?"

"No," replied the other. "Routine stuff."

For him, it no doubt was.

Chapter 9

Rhythm and Character

I have a simple theory that the leading sportsmen and women are born with a sense of rhythm, a sharpness of eye and a keenness of movement that others do not have. These gifts can very easily add up to nothing if you are not prepared to work at them, bring them to their peak.

Much of the golfing polish I acquired came, as I have said elsewhere, from studying such successful players as Bunty Smith, JoAnne Carner and Catherine Lacoste but, had I been looking for excuses not to bother with all the hard work, there were plenty to be found.

For instance, I used to get very frustrated when I heard would-be intellectuals belittling the whole idea of being good at a sport, making out that it was a complete waste of self and time. Much of what they said could be put down to a certain jealousy of the kudos that goes with being a number one, the media attention and the V.I.P. treatment one is apt to get. But such remarks did hurt and more than once had me dwelling on the other things I could have done. In fact, I would like to think that, had I persevered with my school work and gone on to university, I could have been just as successful in another field.

However, even the most sceptical of academics must surely understand that being the number one in golf brings pressures which are apt to stretch one far beyond the mere hitting of a little white ball. And this side of things is, I am sure, appreciated by many of those who come to watch. As the top player, you are mentioned as the likely winner every time you arrive at a championship and, adding to the strain of being expected to be the best, there is often the further dimension that your performance is going to count towards something else.

I think you can win occasionally by surprising yourself. But it's not just the isolated winning of a Scottish championship which counts. It is going on from there to win the British championship and not letting anyone who has never beaten you before get the upper hand. On the same tack, if you are up against someone who beat you the last time, you have to reverse that result in order to show they have not jumped ahead of you. Every match is a pressure match. You need drive, discipline and desire to stay at the top and, as you concentrate on these things, you may antagonise another group of people—namely, your golfing colleagues.

Initially, I used to be happy enough to linger over tea in the clubhouse and to stay at a championship with a group of friends. But, as I got into that higher grade in the game it began to worry me. I wanted then to stay with someone I knew really well, someone who would not be looking to seize upon odd things I had said as sounding big-headed. I began to isolate myself and gradually, as the years wore on, withdrew more and more into myself in certain situations. The expression "It's lonely at the top" is very true but it is my belief that there are a lot of girls—especially in Scottish golf—who are not prepared to accept this.

I was always a little upset by the Scottish players' attitudes when we travelled to events outwith Scotland. As one who saw every championship as a new platform for learning, I used to deem it pointless to play round and round in practice with the people I had been facing in county matches and friendlies back home. Rather, I liked to play with the Lally Segards, the Brigitte Varangots, the Catherine Lacostes and the Marley Spearmans. Partly to see how much catching up I had to do and partly because it was so good for your confidence if you played in such a group and played well.

My fellow Scots' interpretation of all this was that I was "dropping" them. Maybe, if they read this, they will understand that I was simply working on the kind of single-mindedness you must have if you want to be a champion. That said, I would like to emphasise how much I learnt from the attitudes and application of many of the Scottish champions—all of them great characters—who came before me. People such as Charlotte Beddows, Jean McCulloch, Helen Holm, Marjorie Draper, Jean Donald and Jessie Valentine.

Charlotte Beddows was a great lady; very feminine and one who spoke her mind at all times. I can remember an occasion in

86

my second Scottish championship at Elie when I was playing in the qualifying rounds and had Mrs Beddows in the party directly behind. She always had a caddie and was quick off the mark and, at the end of the day, I was a little worried that I might on occasion have kept her waiting. I sought her out and said I was very sorry if I had held her up.

"My dear," she replied, "you didn't just hold me up, you held up the whole course!"

Marjorie Draper was another with a wonderfully wry sense of humour and a lovely way of putting you down if you stepped out of line. There was a time when she was playing in the foursomes in Home Internationals at Porthcawl with a youngster who hit a very long but wild ball. Soon after the turn, they came to a hole where, if the tee shot was a good one, you could go for the carry over a couple of cavernous bunkers with your second. It was Mrs Draper's drive and she hit it well enough to have the youngster hitching up her sweater-sleeves and talking, excitedly, of how she was going to go for the green.

Not just any row of lockers but those belonging to the men of the R. & A. This picture was taken at the British Women's championship of 1975, with Maureen Garrett, left and Cindy Hill of America.

"Just remember," intoned Mrs Draper, "who's going to play the next shot."

It was in that same round that Mrs Draper and the new recruit arrived at a tee where one member of the opposition made the mistake of teeing up her ball a little in front of the marker. The player in question, who had very fidgety footwork at the address, had just begun these preliminaries when Mrs Draper, as only she could do, interrupted.

"My dear," she said, "would you mind playing the whole course?"

The English partnership lost a bit of composure after that, albeit I don't for one moment think that any gamesmanship had been intended. It was done—quite rightly—as a reminder that you should be accurate over such things.

I was fortunate enough to have been a member of the same club—the Ladies G.C. Troon—as the great Helen Holm. I had not applied to join but, shortly after my marriage in 1960, I was asked if I would like to become an honorary life member. Over the years I played there quite often but it was not until the last few seasons, when the handicap regulations dictated that you should have cards over so many different courses, that I started to get involved in club competitions.

They enjoy the story in Troon of how, when I first went to play in a monthly medal, the secretary gave me my partner's scorecard and suggested I should take mine as well. "It's a Mrs English you're playing with," she said, pointing out the lady in question in the car park.

I approached this Mrs English, with whom I nowadays always have a cheerful exchange, and said, "Excuse me, I have the pleasure of playing with you today."

"And who," she asked, "are you?"

In the '60s I played a lot with Mrs Holm, a tall lady of whom I was a little in awe. I was still at the stage where I was standing up and giving the ball a carefree thrash and it was she, more than anyone, who taught me what control and delicacy of touch are all about.

She was none too fit and 53 years of age when she beat me in the 1960 Scottish championships at Turnberry. The sheer brilliance of her touch on what was that week a dry, bouncy course was incredible.

The year before, when I had reached the final of the British Women's Match-Play championship at The Berkshire, she had been generous enough to give me a few words of encouragement at the half-way stage of my final against Elizabeth Price.

"I think you should be a little more careful in the afternoon," she advised. "When you get into the heather, don't go for too much; make sure that you will be playing your next shot from the fairway."

I was two up mounting the tee of the 34th but promptly sliced my drive into the edge of the heather. The lie, when I got there, could scarcely have been better but, remembering Mrs Holm's words, I stopped thinking in terms of a five iron and instead selected an eight. Nothing, I thought, could be safer than that but, to my horror—and heaven knows what Mrs Holm must have made of it—I caught the ball perfectly and hit it into the heather on the other side of the fairway. After that, I had no hope of reaching the green at this par five in three and lost the hole to a five.

The last hole at The Berkshire is a short hole. Elizabeth, who was such a well-schooled golfer, knocked her ball on the green and I had all the pressure of trying to knock it on behind her. Just as I was getting down to the shot, a photographer caught my eye. It was still early in my career and I am afraid I allowed myself to be distracted, missing the green to lose the hole and have us setting out down the 37th fairway.

Sharp cure for slow play

I was delighted to see the English chairman, Sue Johnson, taking a stand on slow play during the course of 1987. However, I think it would be much easier if, in these islands, referees were in a position to take the same decisive action as did P. J. Boatwright in the U.S. Women's Amateur at Canoe Brook, New Jersey, in 1983. Having earlier warned a couple for slow play, he had gone back to see if things were moving a little faster. They weren't, so he took the step of telling the players that he was monitoring their game. Minutes later he went up to one of them as she was going through her pre-shot routine and said she should pick up her ball and proceed to the next tee. She had, he said, taken her forty-five seconds, or whatever.

He did not like doing what he had had to do but, as he pointed out at the end of the match, he was merely adhering to a clear-cut set of rules.

89

There I had no one but myself to blame for a second, a topped three wood, which squirted into heather which reached up to my knees. It has all been trimmed a little now for the sake of visitors paying vast green fees but, at that stage, it was meant to be punitive. I had had it and, as we walked back to the clubhouse, I was still thinking back to the 34th and the fact that my interpretation of Helen Holm's excellent advice had gone so sadly awry.

Jean Donald was an entirely different golfer to Helen Holm: where Helen had a flowing swing, Jean had an economical action with which she dealt the ball a smart clip. I came into golf at a time when she had just turned professional and I was greatly attached to the clubs I had which bore her name. In fact, I used Jean Donald clubs right up until the time when my strength was such that I had to switch to men's clubs.

Jean's record was first-class, but Jessie Valentine's was nothing short of phenomenal in that she collected six Scottish championships and three British. I admired Jessie for much the same reasons as I used to admire Gary Player. She was absolutely tiny but, just as Gary made the absolute maximum of what he had to be able to live alongside such relatively huge hitters as Palmer and Nicklaus, so she worked on a game that featured wonderfully straight hitting.

When I knew her, she wasn't putting quite as well as she had done in her earlier years, but there was still plenty there to be admired. In particular, she had a happy outlook that was almost infectious, although no-one's face would be whiter on the course. I rather think she suffered a lot out there in terms of strain.

I really cannot speak highly enough of Jessie and it was typical of her that when, in 1986, the British Women's Stroke-Play championship came to Blairgowrie, she should have had two of the competitors—Mary McKenna and Claire Hourihane—to stay. And, not content with that, this gamest of septuagenarians insisted on caddying for Claire. It must have been a great boost for Clair to have so knowledgeable and enthusiastic a former player at her side. She duly won the championship and, as you would have expected, paid a marvellous tribute to Jessie's contribution at the prizegiving.

Jean McCulloch, like Jessie, was as game as they come. This former triple Scottish champion was the first of the great women golfers I came in contact with, the two of us having played together on the day after I had gone to Glasgow to buy my original

90

"Jean Donalds". Jean always took a special interest in me because she had won the first of her Scottish championships, in 1913, over Machrihanish. In fact, she later donated her medal to the club.

Though no longer able to drive a car, she still does her share of golf watching. Indeed, I could scarcely believe the journey she made in order to watch the 1986 Helen Holm championship. From her home in West Kilbride she caught a bus to Ardrossan. And at Ardrossan she changed to another bus for the trip to Troon. That set her down at the end of the road and, after walking along to the clubhouse, she had lunch with some friends before setting out to watch the afternoon's play. It was a cold afternoon, but she must have followed six or seven holes before having her tea and heading for home.

Maureen Madill, Mary McKenna, myself and Maire O'Donnell, our captain, at the 1980 World Cup in Pinehurst.

That, to me, is a little story that conveys much of what is best about golf. You can go on for so long, forge real and lasting friendships. I thought of this when I visited the last day of the Commonwealth Games in Edinburgh. To see all the athletes dancing and linking arms round the track was very moving, a lovely experience. But, to be honest, I almost had a tear in my eye, for all too many of those athletes were probably never going to meet again.

Learning from Europe . . .

In July 1987 I was for the first time involved in the European Team championships as an official rather than a player, with my role that of assistant referee at Turnberry to Angela Bonallack.

The various countries—there were 13 of them—had prepared for this major event on the women's calendar in their own ways and to me it was at once fascinating and a little worrying to see them at work. Fascinating in that there was so much to be learned and worrying because there was often the feeling that we, in Britain, are in danger of being left behind.

For example, while we are still clinging to amateur ideals, the Swedes have no such traditions and are unashamedly preparing their girls like so many Olympic athletes. Any girl picked for the Swedes squad has to go along with what the coach and trainer recommend. Either that or she is out on her ear.

These Scandinavians brought a male coach and captain to Turnberry and it was noticeable to everyone just how well the players related to officials not far removed from their own age group.

The positive attitude of the Swedes was borne out in a conversation I had with their coach, Pierre Karstrom, after they had beaten England, the holders, in the first round of the match-play.

"I thought you might win," I volunteered, my feeling having been based on what I had seen on the days before.

"I didn't think we would win, I knew we would win," returned Pierre—and there was not so much as a hint of arrogance in his voice.

If the Swedes always looked a confident crew it had much to do with the fact that their whole routine was designed to have them feeling like champions. In the time leading up to a match they would go through the same process of visiting first the practice ground and then the putting green as everyone else. However, what went on at the first tee was rather different. Where, in those last few minutes, many of the competitors would be talking a little nervously to their team-mates before preparing themselves for the opening drive, the Swedes were given a bit of massage about the shoulders. This, to my mind, was something which must have made them feel as relaxed as anyone could hope to feel at that point. After the massage, each player would have her quiet time as she collected thoughts which had already been well trained by the positive thinking tapes the Swedes so favour.

The Germans had similarly left nothing to chance. At Turnberry they could have tucked into what is probably the best breakfast in the world. Yet they came along with their own brands of muesli, clearly believing they had with them the optimum foodstuff. I asked, lightly, if one packet was for chipping and the other for putting but, in truth, I admired them for that discipline and attention to detail.

Obviously, one wouldn't want to make everyone eat muesli if they did not like the stuff, but how much better it is to have girls thinking in terms of health foods rather than milk shakes, ice creams and crisps.

Under Emma Garcia O'Gara, a leading Spanish golfer turned official who has always recognised the importance of keeping up with the times, the Spaniards had to work like dogs to get into their team.

The same applied to the French who will no doubt be eternally grateful to Lally Segard, a many-times French champion and a former winner of the British, who hauled the women's game in France to where it is today virtually single-handed and who would have to qualify as one of the finest ladies in golf. They had a qualifying event to decide team places and those who played badly in that missed out. It was as simple as that. Maybe we are too lenient on the girls in the way we do things. After a couple of good results our players are able to sit back in the knowledge that they are safely aboard whatever team it is. In other words, the way the system is now they can go to sleep.

The Belgian set-up interested me in that the players work under an ex-Ryder Cup Scot in George Will. He is in the perfect position to be able to make real headway with his charges in that what he says goes. No suggestion from him has to be bandied around at committee level and he is therefore well placed to get things done. Take, for example, what he did with the 1987 Belgian men's side. In his opinion they had not worked hard enough for the Men's European Team championships held shortly before the Women's at Turnberry. He thought about it long and hard and, having decided they didn't deserve to go to Austria, he took it upon himself to withdraw their entry. That, surely, must have made them sit up.

European golfers have long been coming over to Britain to gain experience in our events. To my mind, the time has come when we should be sending players over to their major events. The Swedes, the Spanish and the French—they are all in a position to be able to teach us a thing or two.

Chapter 10

Golf at Fifty

People often ask if I was a better golfer at 50 than I was in my late 20s and early 30s. There was a spell in the '60s and early '70s when I was probably picking up more titles than at any other stage, but I think I can safely say that I was a more complete golfer on reaching my half century.

I had lost a little length but, over the years, I had shrugged off all the shyness that can be so inhibiting. At the same time, I had accumulated a wealth of experience which helped me to keep my bad rounds within the bounds of respectability. In other words, what might have been an 83 or an 84 in those earlier days would probably have been nothing worse than a 76 towards the end of my career.

Perhaps more importantly, I still felt, at 50, that I was going forward rather than back. I had won the British Women's Open Amateur Stroke-Play championship at Formby at the age of 49 and, once I had done that, I felt inspired to try for the Curtis Cup the following year. Had I not won the Stroke-Play, I doubt very much if I would have had the necessary motivation to go through with those long months of winter training.

I tend to go along with the view that it was a lifetime of experience that went into my second qualifying round for the British Women's Match-Play championship at West Sussex in June '86. The Curtis Cup side was to be announced at the end of that week and, though I thought my results had me comfortably within the top eight players in Great Britain and Ireland, I felt the selectors might yet be tempted to opt for someone younger, especially since the match was to be played in the heat of Kansas. Again, if I had been too old at 48 for the 1984 match at Muirfield— I did not even make the short leet—it seemed a little improbable that I could be young enough at 50.

Anyhow, nothing was going quite right for me on that second qualifying day and, when it came to the 15th tee, I heard I would need to finish with four straight pars in order to fill the last of the 32 qualifying slots. I answered that challenge by covering those remaining holes in two under par—two birdies and two pars. I qualified with ease and, I must say, it was immensely satisfying to have proved to myself that I still had the requisite nerve.

It helped that I felt more comfortable on the greens in my last few years than at any other stage in my career. Indeed, when it came to the aforementioned Curtis Cup and I had putts each day on the 18th green which mattered to me more than any others I had had over my 35 years in the game, I was able to make them. A 25-footer went down the first morning and then, on the second, I holed crucially from 12 feet.

In February 1987 I was at a dinner at Buchanan Castle Golf Club where Michael Bonallack was the guest speaker. We got talking about putting and I brought up the fact that he had at one point been the best putter in Britain, amateur or professional. He agreed that this had probably been the case but went on to say that it was a part of the game which had since left him altogether.

He was fascinated to hear how the reverse had applied in my case and agreed that it probably had much to do with the fact that I did not really learn to putt till late on in my career and therefore never knew the strain of having to live up to a reputation in that department. It was not that I had been a bad putter before, because I had always holed out quite well and made my share of six and seven footers. What I had never been able to do, though, was to sink tramliners. I could never, for example, do what Wilma Leburn, née Aitken or Trish Johnson can do with a putter while, in the days before these two, I remember being similarly astonished at the putting feats of such as Joan Lawrence and Ruth Porter, both of whom were apt to dub a day a disaster if they hadn't holed a handful of long ones.

I have mentioned elsewhere how a colleague had pointed out that I should be making more putts and it was after I had thought about her remarks that I read and re-read Tom Watson's theories on putting. From them I worked out that I needed more left-hand control, together with a shorter and firmer swing in which I accelerated more through impact. Also, from what he said, I was able to pinpoint a definite fault in my putting action—one of having half an eye on my putter as I took it back. I followed his advice in determining which was my master eye—my left as it turned out—and thereafter resolved to keep it firmly on the ball.

Watson's views on posture similarly struck a chord. What he said, more or less, was that you had to be comfortable but not contorted. You get little old ladies in funny positions on seaside putting greens who seem to be holing everything in sight but that can never work for someone putting amid the pressure of championship golf. You have to have a simple stance which you can find easily if things should start to go wrong.

Once I had latched on to a positive method I stuck with it and devoted a lot of time to getting it right. Unless I was practising on really good greens, I would never bother with the little putts. What I did was to concentrate on five-footers and on hitting hundreds and hundreds of long putts, dropping balls all the way round the edge of a green.

I mention all this because what worked for me—a complete change of approach at 45—might well work for anyone else who feels she is not making her share of putts. A switch of putter, a change of emphasis, a complete spring-clean. They are all worth a try.

Leading Amateur in the British Open at Wentworth in 1980.

My concentration, at 50, was first-class, although not quite as effective as it had been in those earliest days when I would be in the kind of competitive trance that goes with being oblivious to all the things that can go wrong. In the years between it was often a little fitful. Sometimes I would expect too much of myself, mostly because I would be worried about how this result or that would affect my chances with the selectors. In time, I got accustomed to the fact that you could be at the top of their lists one year and not given so much as a mention the next. And, once I had learned to live with their vagaries, my concentration improved dramatically. For the last three or four years it was consistently good.

It was probably my physical fitness at 50 which, more than anything else, enabled me to live alongside such gifted up-and-coming golfers as Trish Johnson and Lillian Behan, fellow members of the '86 Curtis Cup side.

If you have a fit body you can hang on to much of your length. And it helps if, like me, you started off with a surplus of that commodity. In my earliest golfing days I would be 30 or 40 yards ahead of most of my contemporaries and as many as 50 yards past my great heroine, Bunty Smith.

However, as women in general began to hit the ball rather harder, so I lost some of this advantage. Towards the end of my career I was still as long as, or longer than, anyone in British amateur golf with the exception of the aforementioned Trish Johnson and Lillian Behan. Indeed, it is perhaps true to say that I felt my days to be numbered from the very first time they knocked the ball past me. Obviously, I was nowhere near as long as Laura Davies but somehow, with Laura, you never felt that it was a fair contest.

The loss of length is not purely a physical thing but mental as well. The older you get, the more cautious you become and where, previously, there would have been plenty of situations in which your first thought would have been to have a go, you find yourself putting rhythm first. And that is something which applies to the club golfer, too.

One thing I notice, in particular, about the modern club golfer in my age group is that she is a very much more competitive animal than she was a few years ago. I put it down to the fact that so many more women today have jobs in which they have to be competitive—and that competitiveness spills over into their golf. It is no bad thing because, to my mind, women in these islands have for too long been frightened of being caught trying. Which is

Receiving the 1981 Daks Woman Golfer of the Year from the late Dr Leonard Simpson.

all so very different to the way their American counterparts see things.

Even now, for instance, if I were to set out to play with three club golfers here in Scotland, their opening line would very likely be, ''You're far too good for us''. They are too embarrassed to want to make a match of it and, most probably, would pick up after a couple of shots in a bunker for fear of keeping me waiting. In America, the equivalent women would, for a start, have had ten times more coaching, not having considered such an investment at their time of life to be an utter waste of money. They would then be breaking their necks to make a match of it against someone such as myself. And no doubt making grateful mention of the fact that golf, with its system of handicaps, is a game which allows them so to do.

I can remember having a superb match against an American woman to whom I was often giving two shots per hole, although I cannot, for the life of me, remember who won the dollar or the drink. It was that close.

What I am saying is that it is perfectly possible to be competitive in a nice way. An American would deem it a compliment to be called competitive. Not so her British counterpart who would see it as a criticism and thereafter play down her ambitions—that is if she wanted to remain on speaking terms with the other members.

If, at 50, you want to stay fit for golf, don't think you can do that merely by playing your 18 holes three times a week. You need to participate in a more active sport besides. In my case I trained and, when I wasn't training, I would play badminton. The idea behind this is that you should build up reserves of strength so that a lay-off for illness or injury does not leave you as weak as the proverbial kitten.

This, to my mind, is where the middle-aged man has it over the middle-aged woman. The average man will have played rugby or football in and beyond his schooldays and, as a result, will retain the kind of power which allows him to get past the 220 yards mark with a good drive.

Being the correct weight for your build will similarly help you to hang on to your game. Women over 30 who maybe spend a lot of time cooking and sampling what they have cooked must work doubly hard to keep their bodies supple. If they should lose that suppleness, they will find that their swing becomes restricted and that they lose even more in the way of length.

I have talked, elsewhere, of fitness in general but, when you are getting on in golfing years, it becomes doubly important that you should make the effort to warm up before you hit your opening drive. It takes rather more than merely a couple of practice swings. Ideally, you should head for the practice ground and there, before ever you empty out the practice balls, do a few bends and stretches. Then, threading a club through your elbow joints and across your back, turn your body from side to side as you would in your swing.

My father always used to talk of humans in relation to animals. Not only would he describe many a human's lifestyle as being like that of a turkey being fattened for Christmas, but he would tell us to look at cats and dogs to see how, on getting up, they stretch themselves from limb to limb.

On caddying and concentration . . .

In the British Women's Open of 1987 I caddied for Lillian Behan, a colleague from the 1986 Curtis Cup and a former British champion. Far more so than was the case in my own playing days, I noticed the importance to a golfer of patience and concentration.

It was interesting, too, to be in a position to observe what everyone was doing before her tee-off time. There were those who, like myself, turned on the concentration long before they arrived on the first tee; others who were still chattering away as they hit their practice chips to the putting green.

Laura Davies would fit into the latter category. To me, the way in which she can switch her concentration on and off is a part of her brilliance. However, having sat by the first tee at Troon and watched such as Nicklaus and Watson prepare to hit off in an Open, I am convinced that their way—and it is very much one of unpunctured concentration—has to be best for most of us.

The five-iron shot . . .

The first picture catches me as I am taking my last look down the fairway. The set-up looks comfortable, with nothing tight and tense.

Looking at the top of my backswing, you can see I have made a good, full shoulder turn, while my left knee has turned towards my right one rather than outwards. As I uncoil into the ball you can see that most of my weight has been transferred to the left side and that the weight is completely transferred as I drive my right leg through.

Hector Thomson would have approved of that one. In fact, I must confess to thinking I look rather better with a five iron in hand than with a driver. Which is, of course, to be expected in that the longer the club, the more the imperfections show. For me, the five iron marks the beginning of the precision clubs, those with which I am expecting to get the ball close to the flag rather than merely on the green.

When I'm at my best—and I should say I was at my absolute peak with my irons in the late '60s and early '70s—I have the same mental attitude towards hitting a five iron as I do with an eight or a nine. Looking at the men professionals, they can get that feeling using a four iron or even a three. Women, though, are just not strong enough for that. It's not until we get to a five iron that we begin to have more control.

I know there are those who mock the higher woods but, for myself, I would always advise women golfers to go for woods rather than long irons. They are so much easier for the less powerful citizens to swing. It must be 15 years and more since I first acquired a five wood. My Curtis Cup colleagues used to make fun of me and say, ''Here comes Granny with her five wood!'' However, I knew I was very much better with that club than a three iron—and that though I had a reputation as a good iron player.

You hear a lot of older club ladies professing to like their three irons but, though one does not like to say anything, the truth is that they are kidding themselves. They do not actually hit good golf shots with a three iron; it is simply that they can ''nobble'' the ball a long way, especially in summer when the ground is hard. They would get much more in the way of swing and shot satisfaction if they were to use a five or six wood. Having said that, I must confess that I would never want to play with anything above a six wood. Not because I don't approve of the seven and even eight woods, but simply because I would be looking back, wistfully, to the days when I could do so much with my middle irons.

Chapter 11

The Changing Face of Women's Amateur Golf

I have been in the game long enough to have observed many changes, not least at club level where, when I began, there were clubs dotted up and down the country who would not allow women to come in through the front door.

There are establishments who still cling to such archaic ideas which, as I see it, are based more on selfishness than anything else. Because the men pay higher subscriptions, they see such things as the sole use of the front door and prime tee-off times as their prerogative. Also, you will find that many a man still adheres to that old belief that women, being shorter hitters, are bound to keep others waiting.

Personally, I should like to see women paying the same subscriptions as men. Family membership should be available, as should husband and wife memberships. You would then have men's locker-rooms and women's locker-rooms and the rest of the clubhouse would be open to everyone.

The Continentals will never believe the rules and regulations we have here. In Europe, the men and women often play their medal events together. With so many golfers in Britain, I don't suppose such an idea would be practical but, even if it were, I rather think the mere suggestion would drive most males apoplectic. Yet, to my mind, the things they say about women golfers being slow are mostly so much rubbish. Women on the whole play every bit as fast, if not faster, than men. They maybe will not hurry when they are out on a quiet afternoon for a leisurely four but put them into a situation where they have to hurry and they will.

Having said all this, I must confess that I do not object to those all-male clubs which are so proud of their long-held traditions. Ian is a member of the Glasgow Golf Club and, though I can only play there six times a year, they treat a visitor as a visitor should be treated. Certainly, there is none of this nonsense about women having to go in through a back entrance. That kind of thing is disgraceful in this day and age.

At Troon, of course, there is both a men's and a ladies' club. At the ladies' club you will sometimes hear the ladies saying to male visitors that they cannot go into the dining room without a tie but, as you would expect, the rules the other way about are a bit more stringent.

On the day of Borg's fifth Wimbledon win, I had been playing round the Portland course with Jim Walkinshaw and his daughter, Fiona, who was the first girl to play in the men's team at Oxford. We had finished playing and were about to watch the tennis on Portland's black and white television when Jim suggested we should go across to the clubhouse at Royal Troon and watch it in colour. There was one ex-captain sitting in Royal Troon's lounge. He gave us a warm welcome but, when we ordered tea, a waitress informed us that no women were allowed in the clubhouse until after six o'clock. The ex-captain was more than a little embarrassed and, in a bid to put him at ease, I suggested, mischievously, that the opportunity would no doubt arise for me to get him turfed out of Troon Ladies.

I came into golf towards the end of that era when the game was the preserve of those women who had a lot of time and money on their hands. Ladies' golf had started with women going up to the club in the afternoon for a few holes and afternoon tea and, when I began, the legacy of those times was still with us. The general assumption being that women did not go out to work, so ladies' events were all played on weekdays.

I was fascinated, at the British Women's Open championship at Wentworth in 1980, to meet Joyce Heathcoat-Amory who won five English championships and four British in the 1920s. She had been invited to Wentworth to present the prizes and I was lucky enough to be among those invited to join her party at tea.

Lady Heathcoat-Amory is in many eyes the greatest woman golfer of all time and, listening to her talk that day, I could readily discern the qualities that had made her the player she was. The grace and elegance which had been so much a part of her swing and her whole approach shone through, while I was taken aback by just how well versed she was about the modern game—and that in spite of the fact that she has so seldom appeared at championships in the last 30 or 40 years.

Five Scots in the 9-strong Great Britain and Ireland Vagliano Trophy side of 1981. Left to right: Pam Wright, Gillian Stewart, Jane Connachan, Wilma Aitken and myself.

A long wait

For long years I would feel completely out of it when people started discussing their holes-in-one. Everyone in the family seemed to have had at least one, while my hairdresser, a friend of twenty-five years, had had twelve or more.

It was in 1984, after over thirty years in the game, that I finally broke this particular duck, with my ace coming at the eleventh hole at St Andrews. What added to the occasion was that there were two or three couples, including a couple of Japanese professionals, waiting on the tee. We didn't see the ball go in and, with the couple in front not signalling as wildly as they might, it was some seconds before we realised what had happened. It was a moment well worth waiting for—and not least because the shot in question, a four iron, could scarcely have been better struck.

I also met Cecil Leitch, whose matches with Joyce Heathcoat-Amory so caught the imagination of the golfing public. She was well on in years when we had a few holes together and I can remember thinking that I should maybe take it easy, do my best to keep her in the game. It goes without saying that I found myself being roundly beaten.

I gather that Cecil Leitch had hit the ball hard in her day but, when I came on the scene, it was still not wholly acceptable to give the ball an unadulterated thrash. A recent flick through the press cuttings from my early competitive years confirms my impression that people thought I hit the ball very much harder and farther than had been the case with most women previously. Now, with so many girls hitting the ball so far, you could say the revolution is complete and that we are today a nation of hitters as opposed to swingers.

We also saw changes in golfing attire. In my early days, trousers were taboo. Gradually they became acceptable on the course, but you would not arrive in your slacks, nor would you leave in them. You had to change to go on to the first tee.

Someone introduced what was quite a natty little number in the shape of a lined skirt which had a zip up the back which enabled you to introduce a pleat or tuck it away at will. I remember being rather proud of this garment in that I was able to wear it up to the club with the zip done up and then undo the fastening to let rip with a driver off the first tee.

There were a lot of tweed skirts early on and the image of big golfing women wrapped in tweeds is one from which we have been trying to escape for years. Paradoxically, though, these traditional golfing garments are creeping back into fashion.

We used to have blue tweeds, green tweeds and a lot of plain grey clothes. There were none of the pale colours which abound today, the pinks, the yellows and the delicate greens. Nor did we have skirts or trousers and matching tops. Shirts were mainly plain white and sweaters were self-coloured and a far cry from the glorious intarsia designs you can buy today.

Team uniforms have improved down the years, as have team arrangements in general. I can remember the first time I was asked to play for Scotland, in the 1958 Home Internationals at Hunstanton. Officialdom gave out money for two nights' accommodation but there were no arrangements for the players to stay together. Those who had been in the team before and knew each other well booked into the same place but I remember being at a little guest house on my own and feeling rather out of things. I was in the team but not really a part of it. We did have lunch together and talked during the meal about the task in hand, but there was never any game plan as such.

Nowadays we are far more organised. For a Curtis Cup, for instance, we start thinking about physical and mental fitness and about how to get our games to peak long months before the event. Also, we start operating as a group or a team very much earlier than used to be the case, with one of our great strengths in the last Curtis Cup being the fact that we knew each other so well.

Especially in England and Scotland, the whole character of the amateur game has changed dramatically since the advent of the professional tour. In Scotland alone we early on lost such good players as Cathy Panton, Dale Reid, Muriel Thomson, Jane Connachan and Gillian Stewart, while the English Ladies Golf Association must more recently have been ruing the loss of players like Kitrina Douglas, Penny Grice, Trish Johnson and, of course, Laura Davies.

With Ian, watching the 1981 Walker Cup at Cypress Point.

It only seems like yesterday that I had my first sight of Laura. She was playing against Mary McKenna in the 1982 British Women's Match-Play championship at Walton Heath. I had been told what to expect in terms of the length she hit the ball but I had also been led to believe that that was all she could do; that her short game was virtually non-existent. It was at the 15th hole that I suddenly saw for myself that she had got the lot. She had hit her ball into sand and could scarcely have been faced with a more difficult shot in that there was only a yard or so of green between the bunker's edge and the flag. Even before she hit the ball there was something about the way she settled to it that told me she knew exactly what she was about. Her shot was a beauty, one which smacked of touch and talent. The other thing which struck me about Laura that day was her lovely attitude; she exuded the same compelling calmness and control that I had seen before in Marley Harris.

Sad though it was that someone such as Laura should have been lost to the amateur game after playing in just one Curtis Cup—the 1984 match at Muirfield—I have no hesitation in saying that the whole effect of the professional game on the amateur has been for the good. Where, a few years ago, girls did not always know how much of themselves to give to their golf, they can now be very much more positive in their approach because they know that a lucrative career can lie ahead. They work harder and get better quicker, even if, like Laura, they do not stay around in the amateur game for long.

Though many parents and their children think of full-time amateur golf as the perfect preparation for the professional circuit, I myself am not so sure. I tend to think a girl is very much better placed if she does something else as well, for even the firmest resolve can be eroded by boredom and there are often long weeks between the major amateur events.

While the number of championships is probably about right for players such as Jill Thornhill and myself who see marriage, so to speak, as a first career and golf as the number two, it is not too difficult to understand how Jane Connachan, for one, complained of having felt jaded in her last year as an amateur. She had done everything in the way of making this team and that and no longer felt she was making progress.

In addition to the problem of boredom, the girl who has nothing else to worry about other than her golf will often have real trouble in getting defeat into perspective. She is liable to moon around for days before shaking off the effect of a bad loss and that, in turn, is something which can eat into her overall confidence.

Yet another likely pitfall in hanging around full time on the amateur scene is that a girl can all too easily be tempted into moving across to the professional scene too soon, especially if she is in a situation where she is just failing to make top teams and is feeling a little depressed with her lot.

Finally, I think it is a bad mistake to make it too easy for a youngster, give her too much too soon. If she gets everything on the proverbial plate she will very likely be a little soft. She will have trouble in handling the "down" periods which are an inevitable part of any sport and will have less chance of acquiring that extra bit of grit it takes to win in a tight situation.

In my opinion, a girl should go either to university or college or, if that is not on, find herself a job wherein she can get time off

A celebratory and long-awaited drink from the Championship Cup. I had to wait until 1981 to get my hands on this particular British trophy.

to play. Besides having a second string to her bow, she will learn something of the disciplines that all too many of her full-time golfing sisters never acquire. Her days will have to be properly planned but, providing the enthusiasm is there, she will fit in all the golf she needs.

I admire those who go off to American universities but, were I a school leaver today, I rather think I would not have wanted to do more than one year over there. The reason for this is that I have heard of too many instances wherein the degrees picked up are not readily acceptable in Britain.

Maureen Garner, I feel, got plenty out of the year she spent in Texas after having first been at St Andrews University, while Maureen Richmond, a doctor who played in the 1974 Curtis Cup, similarly got enough out of her 12 months in the States to suggest it had been a thoroughly worthwhile exercise. The benefits are obvious: there is the chance to grow up away from home, good coaching and a dousing in the type of confidence that is so much a part of American sport.

That confidence can make all the difference, but there is a real danger that the odd girl can fool herself into thinking she is a whole lot better than she is. I have seen one or two cases where a girl would have benefited rather more from being humble, from saying ''I'm not really all that good and I had better get down to some practice''. Again, a girl cannot afford to sound as confident over here as she can in the States. It's a case of when in Rome . . . .

The reason for this is best illustrated by my experience in the British Women's Open championship at Gosforth Park in 1981. As I recall it, I was level with America's Debbie Massey after the first round, or if not level then only a shot or so behind. Anyhow, I had done well enough to have the press calling me to their tent to ask if I could win the thing. As far as I can remember, my reply was roughly, ''Hold on. I'll be happy to finish as top amateur.''

When Debbie Massey heard what I had said, she spoke to a journalist about my typically British attitude and said that she could not understand why anyone would want to be so down on herself. The truth, of course, was that I hadn't meant what I had said at all. I wouldn't have been there in the first place had I not felt I had it in me to beat the professionals as well as the amateurs. But the last thing I wanted at that stage of the championship was to have headlines all over the papers reading: ''Belle Robertson thinks she can beat the professionals.'' To have told the world that would simply have added to the pressures.

112

Obviously it is worth doing a full three or four year course at an American university if you are enjoying it enough but, reverting to what I would do, my plan would be to follow a single year out there by basing myself at an English college, with a view to doing my damnedest to get involved in the English training set-up. At least at present the English system outshines that of all the other countries. They have an élite squad and a B squad who get regular coaching and training under the eye of Vivien Saunders, the result being that they are making their players enviably polished and professional. A lot of money is spent in the process and it must obviously rankle when girls see the training simply as a passport to the W.P.G.A. tour. However, there is such strength in depth in England that there will always be some players left behind who, if you like, will become the Jill Thornhills and the Linda Baymans of the future.

An exhibition match held at Dunaverty in 1981 to mark my win in the British Match-Play championship of that year. Left to right: Duncan Watson Jnr, myself, Mary McKenna and Stuart Campbell.

113

I feel that we in Scotland are trailing England by as many as three or four years. We badly need someone who could cultivate in our players a greater degree of pride in performance.

I must confess to having been sadly shaken by our approach to the Home Internationals at Whittington Barracks at the end of 1986. For some reason or another, most of our players are under the impression that you cannot enjoy a match unless it is something of a social affair. I appreciate that Lee Trevino can chatter and concentrate at one and the same time but there aren't too many Lee Trevinos around. What the girls should be looking to enjoy is the sheer competitiveness of a good match.

For myself, I doubt if I have ever had a more satisfying game than that in which I lost to Marley Spearman in the Home Internationals some years ago. For the most part, it was played in complete silence, although I can still see Marley, after I had had a disproportionate amount of success with a thinned shot and murmured an apology, smiling broadly and reminding me, ''That's the game''. No one could tell a better story or laugh more than Marley when she came in off the course but, while she was out there, she committed herself totally. Which is how it should be.

I feel that the younger Scottish players deserve a far better service in terms of advice about such things as when to turn professional, where they should go for lessons and what they should do on leaving school. For instance, Stirling University offer golf scholarships and have done so for some years—but I don't think there is any kind of liaison between the S.L.G.A. and those who run the golf at the university.

The S.L.G.A. and, indeed, all the other national bodies, must be realising by now that they could be hanging on to their young players for very much longer if they were to succeed in steering them towards some kind of further education. But, to do this, they will have to do something to make the golf season and the academic year more compatible. For example, Elaine Farquharson, twice a runner-up in the British Girls' championship and currently a law student in Aberdeen, has had to forego playing in the Scottish championship for each of the last four years because of school or university exams. It is the same for many other students and, this being so, I think that authority's first move should be to alter the dates of the four national championships. That, incidentally, is not my only reason for wanting them changed. At the moment, they are played in May

114

when there is no rough to speak of and the greens are in bad shape. How much better it would be if we could follow the example of the men and play in July. The rough at that time of the year would really be a factor and the powers-that-be would be setting the girls a test which would be very much more in keeping with events of such status.

Receiving the Avia Watches Golfer of the Year award from Jimmy Tarbuck in 1985.

The running chip . . .

I would describe this shot, for which I am using a four iron in the sequence, as a nice, neat little movement. Where my weight is concerned, I have the feeling of sitting on my left hip. The best way of getting across the type of action is to say that it belongs in the same family as the long putt from the edge of the green.

My swing thought is one of taking the club straight back and straight through. My wrists are firm, the reason being that if they should break there is a real danger of "scooping" the ball. I have my hands ahead of the ball and the ball more towards my right foot.

I learnt the running chip during my earliest days at Machrihanish, used it non-stop throughout my formative years and have never stopped using it since. More than any other, it is the shot which has my friends asking questions. A lot of people tend to dismiss my ability with this stroke by saying, "It's easy for her, she was brought up on a links". But, simple though it may look, it is a shot which requires hours and hours of practice. I will never forget the endless stretches I put in at Machrihanish, hitting into the 17th green with Hector. I was playing from ground covered in daisies and buttercups and I can see them now, swimming before my eyes. I used to get throroughly frustrated because there were weeks and weeks at the start when I had no touch, no feel. But it was worth every minute of it, for I think I can safely say that the running of a chip over sun-drenched turf has been one of the best shots in my armament.

Moving a little farther away from the green, I would rarely play the standard "land and bounce" approach at any links. Instead, I reach for a straight-faced iron and hit a three-quarter shot. From about 50 to 70 yards from the putting surface I would take a five iron; from 20 to 30 yards, my three or four iron, playing it almost as I would a putter.

Even if I had quite a steep bank to negotiate—say I had missed an elevated green at a short hole—I would seldom feel tempted to throw the ball in the air, preferring to knock it into and up the slope. To me, there is very much less risk attached to a low, running shot in that there is so little side-spin on it. If, on the other hand, you opt for the very much more demanding high shot with backspin, you can get an outrageous kick if you should hit something on landing.

I find it very difficult to convey to youngsters the "soft contact" you need for a "runner". They are all the time thinking in terms of taking a nine iron or a wedge and hitting it hard whereas, if you knock the ball along the ground with a flat-faced club, you don't need to hit it with anything like the same force. Even when I moved to Glasgow and was doing my practice inland, I would still work at this shot by picturing a links situation in my mind's eye. Never did this work to greater effect than in 1986 when I was preparing at Dougalston for the Scottish Women's championship at St Andrews. When it came to the 13th hole—a crucial point—in my final with Lesley Hope, I was faced with exactly the same 20 to 30 yard pitch that I had been practising. To my relief, I surmounted the pressure and, short of holing out, could scarcely have made a better fist of it.

In terms of crushing an opponent's spirit, the running chip is out on its own. For instance, when it came to the 1984 Home Internationals at Gullane and I was up against one of the top English players, I used the shot five times in my first nine holes. Of those five times I was twice left with a "gimme" while, on the other occasions, I had an easy enough little putt. It was enough to kill my opponent.

Having mentioned the running chip's good points, I feel constrained to point out that there is a drawback. Namely, that it is appreciated only by the connoisseurs in the gallery, all too many of the rest being under the impression that you have had a "head-up" and that the shot was a complete and utter fluke.

Chapter 12

Curtis Cup 1986

Any résumé of the 1986 Curtis Cup would have to begin with our captain, Diane Bailey, who got everything it was possible to get out of her players. A really great captain is a rarity and I have no doubt that hers will be a difficult act to follow. One little illustration of her perception and diplomacy can be gauged from her handling of me. I had been her captain in the World Cup in Australia in 1968, while the two of us had won the Avia Foursomes together in 1972. Yet she treated me exactly the same as she did the rest of the side. I would not have wanted it any other way but I greatly admired her for getting what could have been a slightly difficult situation just right. Diane also has this marvellous knack of getting across what she wants in one-liners rather than lectures. I have spoken elsewhere of how it was the odd remark to each of us that had us pricking up our ears and beginning to think that maybe we were good enough to beat the Americans. She did not "go on" at us on any score. On the subject of fitness, a simple sentence to the effect that she could not stress enough how fit we would have to be was sufficient to have us working overtime in that direction. On the question of protecting ourself in temperatures which soared over the 100 degrees mark, she made sure we had sun cream and sun hats and made mention of how foolish it would be for any of us to get burned.

I have known plenty of teams in which you would think the various players were on opposing sides rather than working towards the same ends. The 1986 Curtis Cup side, though, was wonderfully close-knit, with the friendship and respect we had for one another having been forged during the Vagliano Trophy match in Hamburg at the end of 1985.

The British team which had played so well in Germany, winning 14–10, had nine players where the Curtis Cup needed eight. Obviously, someone had to go. As it turned out, Maureen Garner, who had acquitted herself particularly well in the Vagliano moved to the professional ranks over the winter. That left eight, but there was one switch, with Karen Davies of Wales coming in for England's Linda Bayman. Linda, who should be chosen for the 1988 Curtis Cup, is a great striker of a ball who cares almost too much for her own good. She had been well placed to make the 1986 side for much of 1985 but had a disappointing Vagliano Trophy match and then, still more crucially, failed to qualify for the match-play stages of the British Women's championship at West Sussex.

Karen, too, failed to qualify for the British but had had great success on the American college scene, where she had beaten many of the girls who were down to play at Prairie Dunes. The selectors, very sensibly, felt she could be an asset. She was exactly that. I shared a room with her and listening to her talking about the American girls was most reassuring. We in Britain had read only of their more spectacular feats. She, though, was able to tell us of how so-and-so had had an 85 in some college event and played thoroughly badly. The great thing was that she no longer thought of them as invincible and what she said did not take too long to get through to us. Karen is a level-headed girl who, I think, will turn professional as soon as she leaves her American university. She is still a little shy but has a nice touch of humour and knows what hard work is all about.

To introduce you to the rest of the Curtis Cup cast, Karen was partnered at Prairie Dunes by Trish Johnson, who won the English Match-Play and Stroke-Play championships of 1985. Trish is a likable youngster who can have the hottest of streaks with her putter and who has preceded Karen into the professional game. Her four points out of four in the Curtis Cup were a superb effort, especially for one who had not always made the most of her opportunities when in a winning position in a championship context.

Where Trish and Karen were first couple on the second day at Prairie Dunes, Jill Thornhill and Lillian Behan played top on the opening morning. It's my belief that Jill will be as valuable a contributor to the forthcoming Curtis Cup as she was in this 1986 match where she won three and a half points out of four. She is in great shape physically and is in her element on the big occasion.

Lillian Behan's background is not dissimilar to my own in that she, too, had country connections, albeit her work was as a stable

Not just any holed putt but the one which meant that whatever happened in the last singles series, Great Britain and Ireland could not lose the 1986 Curtis Cup. Mary McKenna and I took one-and-a-half points from our two foursomes.

The Curtis Cup comes to Dunbartonshire. A chance to show the trophy to club and county colleagues.

girl at the Curragh. Lillian, who is now a professional, has a positively regal gait and that look of a champion I spoke of in connection with Laura Davies. It is intriguing that golf to her was only a game until as recently as 1983. In other words, she has only been thinking of being good at it for about five years and is therefore miles behind the players she has joined on the professional tour in terms of the number of practice balls hit. Once she has settled on the circuit and found clubs which are exactly right, I suspect that she will be in the same league in terms of length as Laura. Not least because of all the grooming of horses she did in her days at the Curragh, she has a tremendously strong pair of arms.

The third couple consisted of myself and Mary McKenna. Mary's introduction to Curtis Cup golf had come about in 1968 at Newcastle, County Down, my favourite seaside course. Her reason for turning up was because she had a friend, Vivien Singleton, acting as a marker. She watched a few holes and then—and this is something she can scarcely believe of herself—headed for the beach to have a picnic.

Mary has been a great friend of mine for many years and I am perhaps too close to her to give a fair appraisal of her career. However, I have always been a great admirer of her talent and, in particular, the length she commands with her long irons. In the context of the '86 Curtis Cup match, we added up to a useful pair in that, where the American girls had had little experience of foursomes, we were veterans in this department and knew each other's game inside out.

Vicki Thomas and Claire Hourihane played only in the singles, each picking up a point on the second day. Claire is a wonderfully tidy little golfer who should never be underestimated. After Prairie Dunes she won the British Stroke-Play championship at Blairgowrie and now has a fine record within and without Ireland. Vicki Thomas has made herself a very useful golfer over the years. She has won a handful of Welsh titles—six at the latest count—and in 1986 went on from the Curtis Cup to reach the semi-finals in the Australian Women's Amateur. Like Jill Thornhill and myself, she is a wife first and a golfer second. She greatly enjoys her golfing forays and it shows, even to the point of her sometimes getting too excitable.

On each of the practice days in Kansas we passed a bank where there was a strip across one wall which would flash the time at us one second and the temperature the next. The latter was up to 108

With Tip Anderson, the caddie whose name is usually associated with that of Arnold Palmer but who was good enough to guide me through the Scottish Championship of 1986. The venue? St Andrews.

degrees one day and 110 another. When, on the eve of the match, it was down to 98 degrees, our spontaneous applause was interrupted by a small voice—Trish Johnson's I think— reminding us how, if it were 98 at home, we would be thinking we were dying.

We were an hour late in starting on the first day but, in what must surely have been a good omen for us, the storm that had caused the delay had brought the temperature down to our level. Indeed, when I teed up alongside Mary McKenna for our foursomes with Kim Gardner and Kathy McCarthy, I still had my waterproofs on over my shorts.

My one thought, over my first tee shot, was to make a good contact and, to my eternal relief, I hit a shot which could not have been better had I placed it on the fairway. There was then this wonderful surge of excitement you always get as everyone moves forward off the first tee. My last Curtis Cup was finally under way.

As we went down the fairway, the top group were playing the third. In my view, the fact that there were so many places at Prairie Dunes where you would meet the other players or see the scoreboard had not a little to do with the tingling atmosphere. It was all so very different to a typical links at home where you get nine holes going out and nine back and there are long periods when players and spectators alike feel out of touch.

Another thing which made Prairie Dunes so perfect a venue was that it was a smallish, almost homely club. The staff seemed to like us, while the members, all of whom were genuinely delighted to be involved, did everything they could to make the match a big occasion. In truth, the crowd was the largest I have known on that side of the Atlantic and I was struck by the notion that the whole aura was what you would have got had the match been played, say, at Machrihanish or Dunaverty.

It was lovely for me that the co-chairman of the event, Peter Macdonald, who had played rugby for Hillhead F.P. before the war and golf for Kansas University after it, had Kintyre connections. He did a marvellous job in instilling in the members the feeling that the Curtis Cup was something special, with nothing impressing me more than the way in which he had had the local boys trained for caddying.

The lads were all aged between 15 and 17 and, in addition to the training and talks they were given, Peter arranged a pre-match dinner—something which contributed to their feeling that they were fortunate to have been chosen for the job. The enthusiasm with which they set about their task was very revealing. I told my own lad, David Tweito, that what I wanted from him was that he should keep my spirits up at all times. This he did, while Mary McKenna's boy, who was a good golfer, was able to help with the line of putts.

Jill Thornhill and Lillian Behan finished first on that opening morning, being two under par as they demolished Kandi Kessler and Cindy Schreyer by seven and six. Trish Johnson and Karen Davies made it 2-0 with a two and one win over Danielle Ammaccapane and Dottie Mochrie—and then it came to Mary and myself.

A stroll through the Lady Golfers' Museum in Edinburgh with Janet Seigal, Curator of the Museum at Golf House, New Jersey.

We were one up after the 16th but took three putts to share the 17th. Mary caught trouble off the last tee and it looked very much as if a halved match was on the cards until I holed a 25-footer across the home green. The way in which that long putt went down in front of the clubhouse and the psychological lift we had from being 3–0 ahead instead of 2½–½, contributed to the great atmosphere over the lunch table.

The momentum stayed with us over an afternoon on which Mary and I were given a rest. With each of our first three players recording wins, the scoreboard showed Great Britain and Ireland to be 6–0 ahead before the Americans gleaned their 2½ points.

There was a certain sense of disbelief in both camps that night. I was very British in a radio interview I had to do, in that, instead of talking of a possible win for our side, I simply concentrated on the fact that there was still a long way to go. As a matter of fact, I think that the young Americans genuinely believed that they had had ''one of those days'' and that everything would come right on the morrow.

Because of the late night finish brought about by the early morning storm, we had to eat dinner in the clubhouse rather than at the hotel. Where, at the hotel, the two teams would have dined at separate tables, we found ourselves having to eat together. Things were ever so slightly strained, if not embarrassing. We couldn't talk among ourselves and didn't quite know what to say to the opposition, although I did get one or two of the college girls to talk about their hopes and dreams for the future.

Eventually we were able to discuss the day over a late-night cup of tea in Diane's bedroom. Certainly, we never mentioned the possibility of an American backlash, even if that was an obvious thought for supporters both there and at home. The way in which Diane prepared us mentally for the second day was no different to how she had prepared us for the first, although there were one or two subtle mentions of the possibilities in store. Her chief observation was that another good start would do us nicely.

Before turning in, we had to select what we would wear in the morning. Shorts were called for, but there was a hitch in that some among us only had one pair of uniform shorts and, when we went to wash them, we found all the machines being used by basketball players staying in the hotel. All of which goes to show how a team should err on the side of having too many items of uniform rather than too few. We had enough shirts and skirts but, in those temperatures, we needed shorts for each day if not for

126

each round. In the end, we did go out in shorts but not too many of them were uniform.

Once again we got off to the kind of start Diane had deemed so important since she first studied the way in which matches had gone in the past. She had noted how badly British sides were apt to begin, with things having reached a nadir in 1982 at Denver when player after player lost the first hole.

On this occasion we won the first hole or halved it in every game while, as Michael Williams of the *Telegraph* wrote, our finishing was equally hot. Of the 18 matches, eight went to the last hole and yet not once did Britain lose. There were two birdies, five pars and only one bogey—a set of statistics which, as Williams pointed out, could have swung the whole match by the eight points that separated the two sides at the end.

The history-makers. The 1986 Great Britain and Ireland side which became the first British side—men's or women's—to triumph on American soil. Left to right: (Back row) Clair Hourihane, Karen Davies, Lillian Behan, Mary McKenna, Trish Johnson, Sue Shapcott (first reserve), Vicki Thomas. (Front) Belle Robertson, Jill Thornhill, Diane Bailey (captain), Elsie Brown (vice-captain).

127

There were anxious moments when, after Jill and Lillian had sewn up their point, Trish and Karen, three up with three to play, lost both the 16th and the 17th holes. At the same time, Mary and I were going from three up to one down as Kim Gardner and Kathy McCarthy made three birdies in four holes from the 14th on. Trish came up with a shot of shots at the 18th—an eight or nine iron which finished inside a brilliant American second—to save the situation in their match. Then it was up to Mary and me to salvage what we could from our game.

Mary, as is so easily done, because the fairway slopes sharply to the left, had hit her drive at the 372 yards last into much the same area in the rough she had found the day before. My recovery was pretty good, but it did not reach the green. The Americans, in a moment which had my heart missing a beat, then hit their second too far, the ball disappearing into a difficult area over the back of the green. Mary hit our third to around 12 feet and the Americans chipped up to 16 feet. They then proceeded to putt dead and must have been feeling that their point was pretty safe. I conceded their little one before, taking aim on the right edge of the hole and telling myself not to look up too soon, I made the putt that clinched the half point. It meant that whatever else happened, we couldn't lose the Curtis Cup.

Peter Macdonald was moved to suggest that I might like to do to the 18th green what the Scots had done to Wembley and take a piece of it home. The fact that that putt had gone down did great things for our morale. We were, of course, fairly sure that we would go on to win, even if we did not want to admit as much.

It was a situation which reminded me of the 1971 British Women's Stroke-Play championship at Ayr Belleisle. I had been ahead going into the last day and the lady with whom I was staying, Jenny Wallace, had hurried off to buy champagne that we might celebrate my success in the evening. I made very heavy weather of my final round and, almost inevitably, my poor hostess had a positively wretched afternoon as she blamed herself for having so courted disaster. To her relief, we needed the champagne in the end.

Mercifully, we stayed in control at Prairie Dunes, with Trish Johnson holing the putt that enabled us to do what no British team—Ryder, Walker or Curtis—had ever done before. Namely, to win on American soil.

Over lunch on that second day, Diane Bailey had come across to talk to me about her line-up for the last series of singles. I was still high from having holed that all-important putt and, though I would have been happy enough to play in the afternoon, I think we both sensed that the moment was right to give the younger ones their turn.

What she said was typically economical. "Shall we," she asked, gently, "let you go out on a high note?"

Pro-ams

Unless you get a format such as that in the Hennessy Cognac event, where you have only the one amateur to a professional, pro-ams do little to stretch the professionals. When you get the usual quota of three amateur partners, all of whom will be armed with strokes, there is no reason for the professional to bear down over the eighteen holes.

From the amateur's point of view, though, pro-ams can be invaluable. He can ask his professional for technical and tactical advice, while he will also be perfectly placed to get a real understanding of how and why the professional reacts as he does in times of crisis. What is more, he can pursue his line in questioning over a cup of tea or a drink in the bar.

I refer to the amateur as "he" because it is a sad fact that relatively few women get to play in pro-ams. To my mind, this is something which should be rectified with, for a start, the women's national amateur associations either begging for places for their top girls or even paying for them. I know myself how much that type of schooling would have meant to me in my formative golfing years.

The good bad weather player . . .

Over the years, I was often referred to as "a good bad weather player". I think it was rather more than merely a case of my having had a few lucky breaks on bad days, for I did win a number of titles in truly awful conditions. First to come to mind is the British Women's Match-Play championship at Conway in 1981 while, more recently, there was the 1985 British Women's Stroke-Play championship at Formby.

I have no doubt that my success in this direction dated back to childhood days when I would walk to and from the village school without giving the weather a second thought. The rule from the relevant government department in those days was that you had to be three miles away from school before you qualified for free transport. We were comfortably inside that distance—but it still added up to a fair trek. A whole crowd of us would make the trip together; myself, my brother and a goodly representation from the ten-strong family of McShannons who lived in the cottage on my uncle's farm. We had various stopping points and, especially on the "homeward half", would take our time.

Our first port of call would be the smithy where, if it was a wet day and there was not too much work being done on the farm, we could look over the wall and see the horses being shod. The blacksmith's name was Dougald McCallum and he was known to us as "Big Duggie". In his youth he had been quite an athlete, featuring in the races and tugs-of-war that used to be so much a part of local life. He was a fine, strong man who would be clad in a big leather apron for his work. We would watch, riveted, as he would use the bellows, rake the coals and take the red-hot shoe on and off the fire, giving it a smart bang here and there. That done, he would take the shoe—I can almost smell it now—through to a little room where the horses were waiting. To me, there was always a touch of wonder about the way in which the horse would accept the hot shoe and have it hammered in without kicking or writhing in agony.

Over the road from the smithy there was the meal mill where the farmers brought the corn to have it ground into oatmeal or what we called hash, a more roughly ground compound that was fed to the cattle. We consumed a lot of oatmeal on the farm. The cows would have it in warm water after they had calved, while all the workers on the farm—there were seldom fewer than three men and a couple of girls—would have porridge as their first course at breakfast.

Having watched the goings on and savoured the smells at the meal mill, we would play this exhilarating little game of jumping to and fro across the stream that drove the mill's wheels. Sometimes the horses would join us and paddle in the water once they had had their new shoes on, perhaps because the cold water acted as some kind of a finishing process.

In summer we would fish in Conniglen burn and in the winter we were foolhardy enough to slide across its wider reaches. Almost inevitably, there came a day—in that terrible winter of '46—when the ice cracked. Maybe I had been a little arrogant in going further out on to the ice than the others but there I was, in my tweed skirt and with my satchel on my back, disappearing into the water. There was quite a spate beneath and I shall always be grateful to James McShannon who, along with his brother, had the presence of mind to break the ice further down stream. The two of them then grabbed at my satchel as I came floundering by and hauled me to safety. I can remember, vividly, the tremendous feeling of warmth that came over me before I was conscious of being wretchedly cold and wet and having to make my way home.

It was not many hours after I had arrived back in that state that news came that my older brother was among those stranded on their way home from Campbeltown Grammar School and that he would be spending the night—it turned out to be two—at my school. We did not have a telephone at that time and my father, in order to reassure himself that everything was all right, set off amid the ever thickening snow to see for himself. He was a fit man, but that two mile round trip, in which he had to take his bearings from the hedges and fences, left him totally exhausted. Just as it took conditions such as those to disrupt our

A presentation from Dunaverty—a painting of the course—to mark my retirement from competitive golf. Left to right: June Watson, Win Trappe, Duncan Watson, Hugh and Jan McCorkindale, myself, John Trappe, Roy McMurchy, Marlyn McMurchy and Angus McVicar.

131

schooling so, when it came to golf, we would never have looked out of the window in the early morning to worry about whether or not the day was suitable. Unless there was snow, the courses were always playable in that they were so dry underfoot.

Crae McIntyre and Alan Mackenzie, the two local policemen whose off-duty hours tallied with my between-milking stints, were as oblivious to the conditions as I was myself and many was the time I would arrive back at the farm with my waterproofs sticking to me and water dripping from my hair. With such a baptism I never, at any stage in my golfing life, allowed the weather to impinge on my concentration.

There have been many Curtis Cups on this side of the Atlantic when the press have talked excitedly of how, if the wind were to rise, the Americans would be blown off the course. That, though, is not quite the right interpretation. What can happen in such conditions is that you might break someone whose concentration and approach are not what they should be. The only time bad weather can become a little unfair is in stroke-play where one player can get the best of the day and another the worst.

In the 1984 British Women's Open at Troon, for example, those who had morning starting times had the wind against going out but at their backs coming home. When I set off, however, the wind had switched to south-westerly and I got it against and across on the way out. Then, as I turned for home, so the wind swung round to be blasting directly into my face.

I fell foul of the weather on the second qualifying day as well; but I'm a bit of a fatalist, one who is inclined to think that if things are for you, they're for you and if they're not, you simply have to wait for the next championship. All you can do is give yourself the best possible chance. And by that I mean wearing the most effective waterproofs you can lay your hands on with a view to keeping out not just the rain but wind and cold. If it was particularly cold—I feel the cold a lot—I would have with me a pair of sheepskin mittens two sizes too large in order that I could slot a handwarmer into each. Again, I would do my utmost to get hold of a good caddie. Certainly, he would have to be paid for but, in my experience, it was better to scrimp and save in other directions, for it is in bad weather that a caddie can be at his most useful. He will stop you from getting just too uncomfortable.

People often used to ask of me how I adjusted to playing in the kind of heatwaves you get in an American summer. It was something which had me so worried when I was first chosen for a Curtis Cup over there that I studied the training methods used by Bruce Tulloch, the Olympic athlete. He painted a lovely picture of how when he was preparing to compete in a warm climate, he would sit in a hot bath and further surround himself with steaming kettles. My interpretation of this idea was to go for a sauna three times a week. I don't know whether it helped but, for sure, I never was overcome by the heat.

One area in which I was maybe a little lucky when travelling to hot places was that, thanks to my fair skin, I never felt that insatiable urge some people have to get a suntan. I was always happy enough to wear a hat or an eye shade and to cover myself up with the latest in protective creams.

Too hot or too cold, the one thing you can never afford to do is to say "This is terrible, you can't play golf on a day like this". Do that and you are giving the task in hand less than 100 per cent.

Trish Johnson and Laura Davies, players of the moment on the women's professional circuit, relaxing on the night of the BBC's 1986 Sports Review of the Year. Like me, Trish was there as a member of the winning Curtis Cup side. As for Laura, she had dominated the professional scene in these islands, topping the Order of Merit for a second successive year.

In 1987 Laura won the U.S. Women's Open, while Trish topped the American qualifying school.

RECORD

Mrs Isabella Robertson M.B.E.
(née McCorkindale)

1957 West of Scotland champion

1958 Dunbartonshire and Argyll champion
Scottish team

1959 Dunbartonshire and Argyll champion
Runner-up British Match-Play championship
Vagliano Trophy match
Scottish team

1960 Sunningdale Open Foursomes with M. Moir
Dunbartonshire and Argyll champion Curtis Cup match
Scottish team

1961 Dunbartonshire and Argyll champion
Scottish team

1962 Dunbartonshire and Argyll champion
Scottish team

1963 Dunbartonshire and Argyll champion
Scottish team
Vagliano Trophy match

1964 West of Scotland champion
World Team championship (St Germain, France)
Scottish team

1965 Dunbartonshire and Argyll champion
Scottish champion
Runner-up British Match-Play championship
Vagliano Trophy match (Kiln-Refrath, Germany)
Scottish team

1966 Dunbartonshire and Argyll champion
West of Scotland champion
Scottish champion
Curtis Cup match (Cascades G.C., U.S.A.)
World Team championships (Mexico City G.C., Mexico)
Scottish team

1967 Year off competitive play

1968 Dunbartonshire and Argyll champion
Curtis Cup match
World Team championships (captain) (Victoria G.C.
Melbourne)
Scottish Sportswoman of the Year

1969 Dunbartonshire and Argyll champion
West of Scotland champion
Vagliano Trophy team (Chantilly, France)
Scottish team

1970 Runner-up British Match-Play championship
Curtis Cup team (Brae Burn U.S.A.)

1971 Scottish champion
European team championship
British Stroke-Play champion
Commonwealth tournament (Hamilton, New Zealand)
New Zealand champion
Scottish team
Daks Woman Golfer of the Year
Scottish Sportwoman of the Year

1972 Avia Foursome with Diane Bailey
Scottish champion
British Stroke-Play champion
Curtis Cup team
World Team championship (Hindu Country Club, Buenos Aires)
Scottish team

1973 Helen Holm Trophy
European Team championship (Royal Golf Club de Belgique)
Scottish team

1974 Non-playing captain Curtis Cup (San Francisco G.C., U.S.A.)

1975 Non-playing captain Commonwealth team

1976 Non-playing captain Curtis Cup

1978 Dunbartonshire and Argyll champion
Scottish champion
Leading qualifier U.S. Amateur
Scottish team
Scottish Sportswoman of the Year

1979 Helen Holm Trophy
Roehampton Gold Cup

1980 Scottish champion
Runner-up and low amateur British Open
World Team championship (Pinehurst Golf and Country Club, U.S.A.)
Scottish team

1981 Avia Foursomes with Winnie Wooldridge
Roehampton Gold Cup
British champion
Runner-up and low amateur British Open
European Team championship (Troia G.C., Portugal)
Vagliano Trophy match (Puerta de Hierro G.C., Spain)
Scottish team
Daks Woman Golfer of the Year
Scottish Sportswoman of the Year

1982 Roehampton Gold Cup
Curtis Cup team (Denver, U.S.A.)
World Team championship (Geneve G.C., Switzerland)
Scottish team

1983 European team championship (Royal Waterloo G.C., Belgium)
Vagliano Trophy match

1984 Avia Foursome with Mary McKenna

1985 European Team championship (Stavanger G.C., Norway)
British Stroke-Play champion
Second low amateur British Open
Vagliano Trophy match (Hamburger G.C., Germany)
Scottish team
Avia Watches Golfer of the Year

1986 Avia Foursomes with Mary McKenna
Helen Holm Trophy
Scottish champion
Curtis Cup team (Prairie Dunes, U.S.A.)

1987 McRobert Thistle Award from the National Playing Fields Association (Scotland)